The Game Ranger, the Knife, the Lion and the Sheep

The Game Ranger, the Knife, the Lion and the Sheep

20 Tales about Curious Characters from Southern Africa

STORIES FROM THE VELD (II)

David Bristow

First published by Jacana Media (Pty) Ltd in 2018

10 Orange Street
Sunnyside
Auckland Park 2092
South Africa
+2711 628 3200
www.jacana.co.za

ISBN 978-1-4314-2702-4

Lyrics on page 98 reproduced with kind permission: 'Impi' by
Johnny Clegg © 1982 Rhythm Safari (Pty) Ltd

Cover design by publicide
Black and white illustrations © James Berrengé
Editing by Linda Da Nova
Proofreading by Megan Mance
Set in Minion Pro 10.8/15pt
Job no. 003318

See a complete list of Jacana titles at www.jacana.co.za

Printed by **novus print**, a Novus Holdings company

Contents

Foreword

Amazing, Immortal Characters

ALL THE CHARACTERS IN THIS BOOK are people I have met through the course of my travels. A few I was fortunate enough to meet in the flesh, although most of them, what with so many being dead before I was born, I have met only vicariously.

In my father's house there were many rooms (he was an architect-builder) and most of them were filled floor-to-ceiling with books. They were then, as they are now, my most valued treasures. Wherever my life has led, I have those books to hold at least partly accountable.

I have always lusted after old things, things like astrolabes, old furniture, any old wood, old books. Once I graduated beyond Enid Blyton I found my way circuitously to the likes of Homer (children's edition), W Somerset Maugham and John Steinbeck. I loved, and still do, old stories about old characters, ones that tend to get lost in out-of-print volumes lying on dusty shelves in musty rooms.

These are places mostly avoided by younger generations enraptured by the new, with an innate distaste for the smell of mothballs and the scent of old people. I'm with them there, but if you are an attic rummager you'll know what treasures are to be found among the *drek*. A great story will always remain great, be it *The Odyssey*, *Moby Dick* or *Grapes of Wrath*. They are worth reading and rereading, telling and recounting.

I amassed the *dramatis personae* in this collection over many years. Initially it was with the vague notion of writing full-length books about enthralling characters like Krotoa, Coenraad De Buys and Maria Mouton. However, as my list grew, the original plan morphed into this, a compilation of stories about some of the most fascinating, lesser-known personalities from the past.

People such as Harry Wolhuter and Helen Martins are two that many people will know something about, but only historians and dinner party bores will know their full stories (I have to stop myself when I notice the eyes of my dinner companions begin to glaze over). On the other hand, the likes of Maria Mouton and Coenraad De Buys have been downgraded to mere footnotes in other more learned works.

These stories deserve to be dug out of the attics of our history, given a good shaking and pressing and presented to a new audience. Throughout my research I was intrigued by how the trail of the stories unfolded. In some cases, such as those of cross-dresser Doctor James Barry and bird artist Claude Finch-Davies, I thought I pretty much had the full sum of them before I even started, but more than once I was proved wrong.

In my early years as a writer, most of my research was done in libraries, most notably the National Library in the Company Gardens. Now, of course, it's the internet.

The powerful research tools available today (thank you Professor Google and Doctor Wikipedia) revealed that in many cases the apocryphal version proved to be just a fraction – and often not a very accurate one – of the full story. It reminded me of that doyen of southern African travel writers, TV Bulpin, who was not averse to bending the facts in the quest for a good tale (or, to put it a bit more kindly, preferring the myth over fact).

I discovered that sometimes something similar applied even in the case of Lawrence G Green, that fine and honest chronicler of old southern African tales. Green was a first-rate journalist and adventurer, as well as a tireless researcher. However, in some cases he just did not have access to all the information. Take the case of Doctor James Barry. Even though Green scoured the archives of the Cape, interviewed countless people and delved into family histories, his was still only half the story.

Researchers in England have recently turned up documents from their side of the Atlantic, including previously classified military records which offer new angles to this time-turned story. The same holds with bird artist Finch-Davies, where a chance finding in a university library unearthed an entirely new final chapter to his tragic tale.

Something else that impressed me was how, when I thought it would be nigh impossible to find records of characters from two hundred or more years ago, out would pop the most extraordinary wealth of source material. The Dutch in particular were fastidious record keepers (who knew?). More recently a small army of historians has collated much of this material and made it available to us onlookers.

Holding the fossil of a creature that lived around here some two hundred and fifty million years ago thrills me and enhances my interest in old things. Among the great privileges of my own more pedestrian life, I have met with naturalists, archaeologists and palaeontologists who have imbued my journey with riches way beyond my expectation.

The craft of storytelling goes back a long time, to the age of Homer in the case of the written format, and to the fires of our ancestors out on the open veld in southern Africa. In medieval Europe it was troubadours who were the storytellers, while here in Africa the *isibongi* were both praise poets to kings and chiefs, as well as entertainers to the common crowds.

Storytelling has been central to our consciousness as a sentient species since we dropped from the trees and gripped stones with our wondrous opposable thumbs. I have also been a storyteller since the time of entertaining my family with impromptu performances as a child (whenever I saw the belt coming out I'd break into a song-and-dance routine).

As a travel journalist I have travelled from the Antarctic to Alaska, Hillbrow to the Himalayas and much in between, but now, much like Charles Darwin once his seafaring days were done, I prefer to hang out in my own corner of the universe. Rather than writing about Greeks odysseys or Bornean head hunters, the stories I want to share are about the fynbos, the Afromontane forests and the African bush – stories from the veld.

This is my second book in the series Stories from the Veld. The first was *Running Wild: The Story of Zulu, an African Stallion* but I had not coined the series name when that was first published in October 2017.

I hope you will enjoy this feast of friends because a good story should never die.

– David Bristow
Cape Town, 2018

Harry Wolhuter – The Travails of Southern Africa's First Game Ranger

The saga of the butcher's knife, the lion and the sheep

MOST PEOPLE WHO KNOW THE Kruger Park well will also probably know something about the story of game ranger Harry Wolhuter's knife and the lion skin in the Skukuza rest camp's library-museum (the one with the rhino skeleton outside). Few, however, will be familiar with the full story and it is worth telling.

Henry Charles Christopher "Harry" Wolhuter was a farm boy from Beaufort West. There he seems to have got into as much trouble as a lad could back in '77 – 1877 that is – preferring to go swimming and rowing in home-made boats and hunting "in the sunny veld in South Africa" with his old muzzle loader than attend school, with its attendant thrashings. One day when caught playing truant, his father bound him in a wheelbarrow and had one of the farm labourers push him to his lessons.

When he was thirteen the family trekked from the Karoo to the Reef and the following year Harry began working in a trading store on the West Rand mines. He also acted as postmaster for Maraisburg and there one day he nearly came to grief. He would accept the mail from the Zeederberg coach when it stopped at the hotel next door to the trading store while the passengers refreshed.

In the mail one day was a registered envelope from the mining commissioner with revenues amounting to around £1,000. That happened to be young Wolhuter's last day working in Maraisburg before he left the store to move to Johannesburg. He handed over the mail to the new store keeper and postmaster with instructions to seal it in with the next outgoing delivery.

The new man forgot to do so and so the money did not arrive at its intended destination. Wolhuter was found to have scarpered to the big city and the alarm went out. Five days later a policeman found Harry in a billiard parlour and immediately arrested him. In time the money parcel was located on a shelf at the back of the store in Maraisburg and Harry was released.

In the meanwhile his family had relocated to White River where they opened a store. Harry soon tired of life in Johannesburg and joined them there. At one time there was a serious malaria epidemic and when he himself recovered he toured the area handing out quinine. Arriving at a farm near Plaston he found the place shuttered up and the animals untended.

The self-appointed medical orderly broke into the house where the farmer, Bronkhorst, and two children were in one room, dead, while the mother with another two was in a second room. They were severely ill and cried for water, which he gave them, and then went for help. Having to bury the one teenage girl deeply affected the young angel of mercy.

From then on his life seems to have been punctuated as much as punctured with episodes of malaria. After one particularly severe incident a Zulu man working in the area found him close to death at the pontoon crossing on the bank of the Crocodile River.

He relates: "I feel sure I owed my rapid recovery to my strong constitution, as taking such liberties with a strong dose of malaria would probably kill many people!"

At that time people were not yet aware that mosquitoes were the carriers of malaria and so no one took preventions against being bitten.

During the Anglo-Boer War Wolhuter was one of only nine members of Steinacker's Horse who lived through the frequent and serious bouts of dysentery and black-water fever. On one occasion members of the regiment had to be evacuated to a hospital ship anchored in Delagoa (Maputo) Bay. His bout of "the shakes" was so bad he reckoned it nearly shook the ship out of its anchorage.

A doctor on board had little appreciation of tropical diseases and his remedy was to have a wet towel placed on the heads of the fevered men with instructions to the nurses to rub them down with ice. Wolhuter was lucky to have lived, but not so much as the time he was taken to the military hospital at Waterval Onder. The troops had taken water from a river in which, later, dead horses were found.

"Don't worry about that one," a doctor advised the nurses on an evening round, "he'll be gone by morning." Wolhuter was slim, fit and as tough as biltong and that constitution would save him time and again.

As a young man Wolhuter loved most to go on hunting trips to the Lowveld. He eagerly joined commandos when word was sent out by the Transvaal Government. They were a kind of people's army where each man had to be mounted and armed and carry his own supplies for the duration of a campaign against various "rebellions" by indigenous people in the old Boer Republic.

When the Anglo-Boer War erupted he joined a private regiment raised by a maverick and flamboyant cavalry officer Colonel Steinacker, Steinacker's Horse. Their theatre of war was the Sabi Reserve, the original chunk of land that later became the Kruger National Park. Here they patrolled in the hope of intercepting Boer forces, either hunting for game meat or bringing in arms from Mozambique.

And so it was that when the old Sabi Game Reserve was revived after that war in 1902, Harry Wolhuter was the very first ranger employed by the reserve's first warden, Major James Stevenson-

Hamilton – a man we will meet again among this curious collection of characters from the African veld.

Wolhuter chose Pretoriuskop as his base, owing to its relatively high elevation that would minimise the risk of malaria. His principle task in the early years was to set up guard posts as far north as the Olifants River, then the northern boundary of the Sabi reserve, and to conduct regular patrols to the outlying pickets. The Boers had shot out the game of the area to such an extent that seldom were any large animals seen other than an occasional steenbok or reedbuck. The first elephants seen in the park made a furtive entrance along the Olifants River only in 1910.

Patrols consisted of the ranger on horseback followed by a line of police constables who tended a procession of donkeys. They would be attended by various dogs from the large pack the ranger kept at his home camp, M'timba. These dogs, usually numbering around twenty at any one time, were all close to wild and were what Wolhuter describes as "lion dogs".

August of 1903 found Wolhuter on the return leg of a patrol to the Olifants River with three policemen in his posse and three "Boer dogs" (mongrels usually with mastiff, ridgeback and terrier strains). It was afternoon in the dry season and they were making for a waterhole some thirty kilometres distant. Wolhuter knew the trail well from his days with Steinacker's Horse and decided to ride ahead in order to get to the water before dark. One dog named Bull followed its master while the other two remained with the pack train.

Darkness fell and the ranger kept on towards the water as they'd had none since leaving the Olifants early that morning. The rider gave no heed to predators because he had not before seen any thereabouts. Also much of the grass and herb cover had been recently burned. So, when he heard two animals leap out of a patch of long grass, he assumed it was reedbuck which he knew liked to lie up in the long grass along the Metsimetsi River.

However, when he heard rustling approaching he knew instinctively it meant trouble. It was two fully grown male lions and they were readying to pounce.

Wolhuter had no time to draw his rifle from its scabbard as the lions closed in for the attack. He turned his horse tightly round and dug in his spurs. One lion was already so close the horse had no time to spring off as the carnivore leapt up. "I felt a terrific impact behind me as the lion alighted on the horse's hindquarters."

The horse bucked and plunged and finally broke free, but not before sustaining severe wounds and knocking the rider from his saddle. His rifle went flying and the ranger landed on top of the second lion that was making to seize the horse by its head. The horse fled off into the night with the first lion in hot pursuit and Bull running and barking after it, while the second lion grabbed and bit down hard on Wolhuter's right shoulder, then started dragging him towards the dry Metsimetsi riverbed.

The lion's claws kept raking wounds into the man's lame right arm as it walked. Spurs on Wolhuter's boots acted like brakes along the stony ground which would cause the lion to give impatient jerks, causing more excruciating pain and lacerations.

"I certainly was in a position to disagree emphatically with Dr Livingstone's theory, based on his own personal experience, that the resulting shock from the bite of a large carnivorous animal so numbs the nerves that it deadens all pain; for, in addition to this was the mental agony as to what the lion would presently do with me; whether he would kill me first or proceed to dine off me while I was still alive!"

Then, through the pain, the prey remembered his knife. A problem was that it had never fit snugly into the sheath on his belt and twice previously it had fallen out when he'd taken a spill while galloping after game. What were the chances it would still be there after all the commotion of the previous few minutes.

The reason the knife did not fit as well as it might was that it was not the original knife he had bought with the sheath. Once when Wolhuter was visiting a friend at his store in Komatipoort he saw a much better but similar looking knife lying next to a wheel of cheese. He reckoned a fine meat knife was too useful to be wasted cutting cheese so he made a quick swap. It seemed too much to expect it would still be fastened in its place.

Working his left hand around behind his back while the lion was dragging and tugging him, his fingers found the knife still snug in its place. The rag-doll man eased it out and then wondered what would be the best strike, as he knew he would have only one good go at best. A heart shot would be most effective and so, with his head pulled hard against the lion's mane, he felt carefully for its shoulder. He was at the same time overwhelmed by the powerful stench of the lion's breath and amused by the fact that it was purring extremely loudly.

The victim then had to stretch across the predator's chest to locate its left shoulder without provoking any reaction from the fearsome cat. Feeling his way and knowing where the heart was, he struck twice as hard and quickly as he could with backhanded jabs. The lion roared furiously. Wolhuter then stabbed at its neck and must have hit the jugular vein because immediately he was drenched with gushing blood.

The wounded predator released the man and slunk off into the darkness. Wolhuter could hear it moaning somewhere off in the distance (he later measured the lion had dragged him about sixty metres). Then he remembered there had been another lion. It had likely run after the horse but if it had not made the kill would soon return to find its accomplice and join the feast (and slim pickings those would have been, the stricken ranger had the good humour to note).

Wolhuter tried to start a veld fire, clenching a box of matches in his teeth and using his left hand to strike the matches, but dew had fallen and a flame would not take. By this stage his right shoulder and arm were punctured, torn and useless and the lion's claws had torn out tendons from his forearm and wrist.

A tree, he would climb a tree. There were several around but it took some time to find one that had a convenient fork into which he could hoist himself and then clamber further up, reaching a bough about four metres up (a lion at full reach will touch three metres; a short leap would having it sitting beside the ranger).

Wolhuter was beginning to succumb to loss of blood and shock but managed to unhitch his belt and tie himself to a branch to prevent himself from falling to the ground. Furthermore his clothing was soaked with sweat and lion blood. He was shivering with cold and still bleeding himself.

The second lion did return and soon located the man in the tree. Having seen off one, was he about to fall prey to another? But as the predator was reaching up towards the man, Bull the "lion dog" ran into the scene and starting yapping and snapping at the cat's legs. Off the two ran into the night playing tag. Eventually Wolhuter heard the far-off tinkle-clinkle of tin dishes rattling in their bags fixed aside the donkeys.

He shouted a warning to the policemen about the lion. They fired shots into the air and then approached their wounded comrade. He told them to first make a fire and then give him some water. A fire they made but they had no water so they all set off for the intended waterhole, brandishing firebrands.

The remaining lion followed just out of sight with the three dogs making darting runs at it to keep it at bay. The waterhole was located at an old guard station from Steinacker's Horse. There was a hut for shelter but the hole held no water. Wolhuter realised he needed water or he would surely die so he sent his men on a life-saving mission to find some.

They returned with a canvas bag filled with muddy sludge. It would have to do, so Wolhuter sucked up as much as he could. He remained in the guard hut all the following day while his askaris went off to find the dead lion and the lost rifle.

Wolhuter knew they would not believe he had done the deed until they found it and returned with the skin, the skull and its heart punctured by two stab wounds. They told him they had found the lion's stomach quite empty, indicating it (and probably its partner too) had not eaten for several days and would have been murderously hungry.

With them they also led the runaway horse, which had returned to the scene of the fight to find its rider. After salt was rubbed into its wounds it was physically in passable shape but never again could it be ridden in game country. Had Wolhuter thought to have salt rubbed into his own wounds, it would have saved much of the pain and hardship that was to follow.

With his condition deteriorating and being unable to walk or ride, the policemen set off to a local village to commandeer help.

At that time there were still numerous small communities living in game reserves before evictions started to clear the area of all human settlements (evictions which in recent times have prompted various community land claims in and around the park).

The wounded man was loaded onto a hammock hastily constructed with poles and a blanket and by and by he was carried village to village by relays of four men at a time, with two assigned to carry water in calabashes. The rough journey to Komatipoort took four days, during which time Wolhuter had no medication, least of all painkillers. He fell into a fever and his wounds turned septic. The smell became so bad even he had to lie with his head turned away from the mutilated, gangrenous right shoulder.

The doctor in Komatipoort cleaned the wounds as best he could but had no morphine to dull the pain that was by that stage literally killing the patient. An old friend from Steinacker's Horse got Wolhuter to the Selati railway and accompanied him to the hospital at Barberton where, finally, proper medical care was provided. However, not for the first time in his life, the medical staff there despaired for his chances of survival during the many weeks it took him to recuperate.

"Once again, however, a sound constitution saw me through, and although I have never since had the full use of my right arm, I consider myself extremely fortunate in not having lost it altogether. As it is, I can still, with difficulty, lift it high enough to pull the trigger."

His boss, Stevenson-Hamilton, in his own autobiography, described him thus: "Tall, spare, but powerfully built; purposeful, for all his quiet voice and unassuming manner, he seemed emblematical of the best type of pioneer hunter."

What is perhaps surprising is that these men, the first generation of Kruger Park rangers, with the exception of a few determined bachelors, eventually found women willing to marry them and share their rough and lonely lives in camps consisting of little more than a hut or two, in the hot and malarial Lowveld all set about by fever trees and wild beasts.

The faithful hound Bull, who without doubt had saved his master from being pulled out of that tree and eaten, found his own end in a battle to the death with a baboon in which both animals died.

"Each of them, in common with many other unrecorded dogs and horses – faithful and staunch companions of the men in the veld – played their part in the achievement of the present-day world famous Kruger National Park and all of them deserve their small tribute."

That was written in 1948, by which time Wolhuter had retired and his son Henry, in his place, eventually becoming head ranger. He was in turn followed by his own son Kim who grew up in the Kruger Park and became a game ranger before moving on to become a celebrated wildlife filmmaker.

Wolhuter's final word on the matter is that: "It was a hard life: full of risks, but we were compensated by the interesting things we saw and did." Wolhuter was not a man much given to exaggeration or self-aggrandisement.

Some years after the lion incident, Wolhuter took a holiday to England. He decided to pop in to see the makers of his life-saving knife. It was a butcher's "sticking type" knife with a six-inch blade made by T Williams of Smithfield in London. He thought they might be interested in his tale, and he could buy a few more to take back home where good knives were hard to come by.

He was met by a "bright young gentleman" who looked him up and down disdainfully. You can imagine the colonial game ranger was not attired exactly for Pall Mall Street in the Edwardian fashion. Wolhuter informed the clerk that one such weapon had once killed a lion and asked if he could buy a dozen.

"Oh yes, they are good. They will also kill a sheep you know," replied the aforementioned young man.

Some time later Wolhuter received a package from London. It contained "a most beautiful knife", a gift from Mr Williams himself, which remained a proud treasure of the game ranger. It was a forerunner of multi-tool knives that today any game ranger worth his khakis wouldn't be seen dead without because, who knows, one day any one of them might have to kill a lion with it.

On my first holiday to the Kruger National Park, the sighting that impressed me most was the skin of a lion and a sheath knife mounted behind glass in the small museum at Skukuza rest camp. I was already familiar with the adventures of Jock, that great bushveld dog. I wanted a dog like that, and a rifle, and a knife.

Our parents bought each of us three boys a pocket knife from the gift shop. They had pictures of the "big five" on the bone handles. I was quite sure I could kill a lion with mine, or at the very least a sheep. Years later I found a copy of Wolhuter's memoirs on my parents' book shelves. I wished I could have grown up in the Lowveld, with a sturdy pony, a reliable rifle and a dog named Jock.

Anthony Hall-Martin – Addo Babies

A human baby meets an elephant baby in Addo Elephant National Park

HUNTERS, THOSE SEEKING THE HEAVY front-end appendages of Africa's giants, were the vanguard of colonial expansion from the Cape Colony during the eighteenth century. It was very easy to follow the elephants eastwards, first over the Olifantshoek (now Franschhoek) Pass, across the rounded hippohumps and rhinorumps of the Overberg, through the dry confines of the Little Karoo and eventually down the Longkloof to the fertile coastal belt towards Algoa Bay where Port Elizabeth lies today.

All you had to do was follow the time-worn paths. Everyone and everything else used the elephant migration routes for their own passage, and it was these same tracks that later became the first wagon roads and, by and by, the byways and then highways of the colony. Game numbers in the nutrient-poor fynbos of the Western Cape were never very high. However, when the ivory hunters reached the Zuurveld region of the Eastern Cape they found the place teeming with not only elephants but also rhinos, buffaloes and other big game.

The portion of the sourveld we call Addo was particularly well stocked but hard to penetrate. It consists mostly of dense thicket, all thorns and spines of the Valley Bushveld ecosystem. What makes it so attractive to animals is the prevalence of a certain plant that the Dutch Trekboer pioneers named spekboom, or bacon tree, otherwise known as *Portulacaria affra*. It is to elephants what catnip is to fat tabbies. It is ridiculously juicy and nutritious (and adds a delicious tart crunchiness to salads, much like clover stems). For good reason it became notorious as a hellish place to track large game.

You wouldn't want to have to track a wounded pachyderm through there with a front-loading blunderbuss. The odds would be stacked heavily in favour of the animals, elephants in particular being extremely canny creatures.

The wagonloads of English settlers who followed the Trekboers also avoided the dense thickets. Addo Bush, as they called it, in time became encircled by farmers who trapped the elephant herds inside what was to be their last refuge in the Cape.

Fast forward to the closing days of the Great War when the Union Government created an irrigation scheme in the Sundays River Valley bordering Addo.

At this time, the problem for the new farmers in the area was that the elephants loved succulent crops and none more so than the citrus orchards that sprung up all along the valley. It is near impossible to keep an elephant in or out when there are orange groves to be raided. Compounding this was the fact that the Addo Bush was almost devoid of surface water.

The inside of an orange is one thing, juicy and sweet, but even when every droplet of juice has been squeezed out and even the oils from the skin have been extracted, elephants will devour the virtually tasteless pith as if it was elephant candy. The pith – the white part – is just as rich in Vitamin C and other nutrients as the fruit. It is also flush with pectin. Elephants soon find out that for them it has the function of greatly improving their normally dismal metabolism. Just look at a ball of elephant dung to see how much undigested plant matter there is.

The Sundays River farming community was not much impressed with this bit of digestive knowledge and petitioned the administrator of the Cape Province to do something about it. The government turned to the hunters but most of them refused the assignment into the "hunter's hell" of Addo. All but for a Major PJ Pretorius fresh back from haranguing the German forces in East Africa alongside the even more illustrious hunter FC Selous.

Pretorius was already famous as the man who had discovered the secret hideout of the German raider *Königsberg* in the steamy mangrove delta of the Rufiji River, so he was no stranger to working in sticky situations. Those of a certain generation will remember the recounting of this story in Wilbur Smith's rollicking *Shout at the Devil*.

The demobbed major took on the onerous business of ridding the Addo Bush of its troublesome elephantine raiders. For the task he had a full-length leather coat made. The official documents record that he shot ninety elephants in eleven months. His own memoir put the figure at a hundred and nineteen.

Whichever is correct, after a year on the job he had had enough of the slaughter and joined the growing group of people who wanted to save the region's last elephants. At that stage there were only an estimated sixteen left, sixteen of the shrewdest, angriest members of their tribe on the continent, and with good reason.

In 1920 a tract of some two thousand hectares was set aside for the purpose of conserving the last Addo elephant herd and a game ranger installed, but it was impossible to keep his charges inside their protected area. As fast as the herd bred, so individuals were shot. Three decades later the elephant population of Addo had increased by just one. The resident ranger had long given up trying and had taken to running his own cattle herd in the reserve.

When Addo became a national park in 1931 its first warden, Harold Trollope, took the job of herding his charges back into their sanctuary more seriously. His successor, Graham Armstrong, went a step further, constructing an all but elephant proof fence using the cables from defunct gold mining head gear as wire and disused railway tracks for posts.

From that time to this, only one elephant is known to have

breached the line, the legendary bull Hapoor. Now the problem was what to do the traumatised and angry residents of Addo. That job fell to a new generation of game ranger in the body of a tall, slim, young researcher named Dr Anthony Hall-Martin. In time Hall-Martin went on to become one of the most knowledgeable and respected elephant conservationist in Africa. With artist Paul Bosman he authored the exceptional monograph *Elephants of Africa*. It sits proudly among the first editions in my bookcase.

When Hall-Martin first visited Addo in 1964 as a post-graduate student, there were thirty-five elephants known to live there, but they were hard to find. Oranges had to be set out around the park headquarters to lure them into the open. When Hall-Martin returned as a research officer in 1976 the herd had grown to seventy-seven but all were wily and cunning, and the born-frees had learned from their elders to be extremely wary of *Homo sapiens*, even those bearing gifts.

The research ranger was there to make observations and collect data, but his subjects proved to be most uncooperative. Hall-Martin's first encounter was with a herd of massive beasts led by a matriarch named Patsy. It ended with an honourable and hasty retreat in his Land Rover before the phalanx of charging *Loxodonta africana*. The rest either kept well out of sight or charged on sight, en masse.

But work had to be done. The next time Patsy's herd charged he backed off, but only far enough to arrest their momentum. The elephants stopped in a shower of dust, then hopped from foot to foot, unsure what to do next, trumpeted and bellowed, then began milling around. When the youngsters started feeding the rest of the herd relaxed and also started feeding.

The ranger repeated this strategy with each matriarchal herd in the park, and then one by one with the bulls until they all began to accept his close presence. Now the serious work of a large herbivore researcher could begin. In time Hall-Martin got his doctorate, got married and with his wife, Catherina, began a period of productive and blissful bush life. All but for a few incidents involving a certain bull named Peet.

On one occasion when in musth – a condition of hormonally charged sexual excitement – Peet attacked and killed a rival bull, breaking one of his tusks in the fury of battle. On another occasion he attacked a herd matriarch, which in itself is extremely aberrant behaviour.

Her name was Catherine the Great and Peet had pounded and gouged her repeatedly, breaking his other tusk in the process. She was one of the eleven surviving females from when the park had first been proclaimed five decades earlier. When the carcass was examined fragments of ivory were recovered from the wounds to the matriarch's neck and shoulders.

Husband and wife watched as Catherine's herd appeared out of the bush in single file and surrounded their fallen comrade. Some tried to lift her with the tusks and trunks (most of the females in Addo are tuskless or close to). Others sniffed and fondled her with their trunks. A blood-splattered calf squealed pathetically, trying to suckle. What else was this but anguish and mourning?

The long game of science is to collect data sets over time that reveal otherwise hidden patterns. Such as the fact that, from the time of the park's founding in 1921 with just eleven survivors, a total of three hundred and seventy elephants had lived there – give or take one or two. The average age of first-time mothers since then was thirteen and by the age of sixteen some ninety-five per cent of females had delivered at least one calf. By the end of Hall-Martin's tenure there, nearly every living cow younger than fifty was either pregnant or lactating, with the exception of maybe one or two.

Eventually the Hall-Martins moved on to Skukuza in the Kruger National Park where he took up the position of head of research for National Parks in South Africa. From there he moved to director for southern parks. The good doctor eventually left the parks board to co-found African Parks. It is a noble and committed organisation that takes the neglected and forlorn of African conservation areas, the drunks and addicts, the homeless and tempest-tossed if you like, and breathes new life and hope not only into the reserves themselves but also the neighbouring communities that have few other resources between reaping the crumbs of tourism and destitution.

It was while Hall-Martin was still in the role of director that I caught up with him at Addo when it was being greatly expanded via corridors to the Zuurberg National Park in the north and Alexandria coastal forest to the south. This swelled the size of the elephant reserve to around fifty-five thousand hectares and negated his great dread of one day having to order the culling of elephants he had come to know so well.

It was easy to recognise his lanky frame, wide-brimmed hat (usually with a handkerchief tucked in at the back to cover his neck) and thin leather gloves in the veld. He was a ginger and the African sun was cruel to his fair skin. You could also tell he was a boffin by the clutch of pens on one shirt pocket and a notebook in the other.

Around the campfire one night he told me a remarkable story that had occurred there years previously. He swore me not to write it as he planned to do so himself when he wrote his memoirs. Due to that promise I did not commit all the finer points to memory. I believe I now have a mandate to tell it, but, since our conversation occurred many years ago I hope I can do it justice. To the best of my memory it happened something like this ...

While walking in the park one day with his family – little daughter Vega had only recently been born – an old female elephant that the Hall-Martins had got to know well approached out of the bush. She was the most relaxed of all the adults in the park. It might have been on account of never having been known to reproduce, or maybe just a personality trait.

When the ranger saw her he had a pivotal moment. "Well I thought if I am going to do this thing properly ..." and he presented his baby daughter to the old matriarch (I do not recall if wife Catherina was there or not. Can you imagine: "Umm, darling, I had a small accident out in the bush this morning ..."). The elephant approached, sniffed and caressed the little girl.

I do have a reputation for having something of an elephant's memory myself, but every time I run the story through my mind things go blurry. Did I dream up this part or not? Because I have a mental movie of the old grey female picking up the baby human and presenting it to each of her own herd in turn.

The next part, however, I am absolutely sure of. The supposed barren female elephant, the one that had never been known to reproduce, went off back into the bush, baby Hall-Martin safely back in her dad's arms. The elephant returned moments later pushing a newly born calf ahead of her and introduced her own teeny baby to her new human friends.

"It was one moment of pure magic in all my years as an elephant researcher," my host recalled in the red glow of the fire. "I cannot explain it but from that moment I knew, I know, just how sentient my subjects were."

Anthony Hall-Martin never got to write this story himself. The merciless African sun finally breached his defenses and he died of cancer in May 2014. I did not get the chance to check the facts with him but I'm not sure it matters now. What does matter is that he left a legacy that will, hopefully, ensure that his as well as other people's children and grandchildren get to see, some even to know, Africa's elephants in the wild just like he did.

The Sad Story of Krotoa or Mevrou Eva van Meerhoff

Colonising and decolonising history and her story

SAILING SHIPS HAD BEEN DROPPING anchor in Table Bay for more than a century and the indigenous Khoisan people living there had become quite used to dealing with them and their needs – fresh water, fresh food and general R&R in that order. To the locals whose lives were dictated by the slow rhythm of the seasons, these strangely dressed white folks would have seemed to be always in a hurry, their agendas driven by the much more importune gyrations of winds and stock prices back in Europe (not much has changed in that regard over the interceding years).

However, when three ships in full sail appeared on the northern horizon in the mid-seventeenth century, the local Khoi people watching their approach could not have imagined the changes to come. The ninety-odd Dutch soldiers and sailors aboard the *Dromerdaris*, the *Reijger* and *Goede Hoop*, their servants and slaves, some of them with their wives, believed it was to be a short assignment (around a hundred and thirty souls did not survive the voyage). They were all wrong: it was the beginning of a new order.

Imagine how perplexing it must have been to the sunburned ears of new arrivals, the clickity-clackity, throat-clearing, cork-popping sounds of the Khoi language and its various dialects (although, to be true, Dutch is no stranger to the hard, guttural, throat-clearing uvular fricative). In the grand colonial tradition, the Dutch were no more likely to try to learn the local lingo than they were to smear themselves with sheep fat, wear animal skins and take to scavenging meat from washed-up whale carcasses.

Even today, some three centuries later, shamefully few white people have learned to speak anything more than a few words of any of the ten official African languages – other than Afrikaans that is. It was called kitchen Dutch but it was really more akin to Flemish and did not sound any more like Dutch than it does now. The irony is that, in the intervening years, descendants of the Khoi have embraced this kitchen Dutch or "kombuis taal" as their own.

Johan (Jan) Anthoniszoon van Riebeeck, his wife Maria de Quillerie and their fellow wayfarers first placed their white-stockinged feet ashore, below the emblematic flat-topped mountain, on 6 April 1652. This is the date usually recognised as the beginning of South African history in the sense of being the written record.

Jan was given the title of commander because, as already alluded, the Cape enterprise was only ever supposed to be a resupply station, there would be nothing and no one to govern. The highest military rank there was sergeant. It was only the unforeseen arrival of French Huguenots some twenty-five years later that caused the small settlement to suddenly swell during the tenure of Simon van der Stel, who was then awarded the title of governor.

Back to Van Riebeeck, whose first order was to construct a fort. Second was to begin procuring food supplies to provide for passing ships; meat should be obtained from the local Khoi and fresh fruit and veg they would have to grow themselves. The Dutch East India Company (VOC), for whom they worked, wanted first of all to secure its assets. The original fort was built from timber cut on the mountain and clay. This was to be their home until the more solid stone Kasteel de Goede Hoop was completed in 1679. (To do the heavy lifting of building a fort and starting a market-garden type farm, slaves were imported from all along the route between Europe and China.)

Lucky for the Dutch settlers, leading the local delegation that came to greet them on the beach was a man who had been abducted some years previously by a Dutch ship, taken around the world and taught to speak their language. It proved to be a godsend for the new settlers in their need to barter for things, most importantly fresh meat on the hoof for the passing ships of the VOC, the world's first multinational corporation. They knew him by reputation as Herry.

Once the Dutch had got themselves settled Van Riebeeck asked Herry – who we shall henceforth know by his real name, Atshumatso – if he could provide someone to work for them in order that Maria would not have to callous her delicate pale hands with all the washing, cleaning and gathering of wood that came with starting a new settlement in Africa.

Atshumatso duly arrived impelling a girl ahead of him who was around eleven at the time. Her name was Krotoa, pronounced Krotwa, and she was his niece. The Van Riebeecks renamed her Eva.

We will never know what arrangement was made between the Khoi headman and the Dutch commander but it goes to the very heart of the matter. Whether she went willingly, attracted by the shiny Dutch cutlery, delicate lace trimmings and fine food, or whether she was coerced, abducted, effectively sold into slavery for bread, brandy, beads and tobacco, is a matter of open conjecture.

This fine point has become a touchstone for reconfiguring our national narrative, what has come to be termed the decolonisation of our history. Was Krotoa the first slave of the Cape, and also the first indigenous concubine of the settlers, or was she a free and willing agent? We don't know and probably never will because facts are thin on paper. Still, that has not prevented anyone with a political dog to walk to discharge on the matter.

In the course of her life that followed Krotoa shuttled between the Dutch outpost and her own people, swapping her fine linen skirts for skins, assuming the guise of either Krotoa or Eva as the situation demanded, such as when she absconded to the Saldahners to mourn the death of her sister during the tenure of Van Riebeeck's successor. This bipolar cultural identity crisis almost certainly caused anxiety and very possibly trauma for the young woman, as the course of her life vacillated between a new bay of good hope and a stormy cape.

During her time living at the fort Krotoa not only adopted the European lifestyle, but around the age of eighteen she became betrothed to a Danish ship's surgeon, Pieter van Meerhoff (some texts of the time use the word "concubine"). Given the lack of single women in the Dutch settlement, this was likely only a matter of time, but once again it is being asked, was she a free and willing participant, or was she the victim of sexual slavery? Was it a deal made between men in which a young brown-skinned woman had no say? Possibly, probably.

Krotoa quickly learned the language of her new hosts and soon replaced Atshumatso as the principal interpreter and guide for her Dutch masters in their dealings with her Khoi kinsfolk. At that time there were about twenty Khoi clans that would have had contact with Europeans, but three are central to the drama.

One, the Goringhaicona of which both Krotoa and Atshumatso were kin, lived almost permanently around Table Bay and over time moved their rudimentary huts ever closer to the fort. In material terms they were the least useful to the Europeans, having few and often no stock animals to spare, living mostly by beachcombing. The Dutch called them watermans or strandlopers.

Their close relatives the Goringhaiqua were more prosperous and lived a little further inland, around what we now call Wynberg and the Cape Flats lakes. The Saldahners or Cochoqua, were the most prosperous of all but they lived far to the north and locals had to be cajoled, paid and generally sweetened up before they would undertake the journey to Langebaan to barter for cattle on behalf of the Dutch. Wire, nails, copper ingots, beads, tobacco (which the Khoi called "dagga") and brandy (known as Cape smoke) were the preferred currencies.

Allow me a short anecdotal diversion here, about the significance of trading beads. They are generally regarded with derision by people of European descent and a sign of the gullibility on the part of indigenous people, but little could be more wrong. Like red hematite, or iron-oxide clay, beads have been used in southern Africa for religious rituals since the time our ancestors learned to make fire and hunt four-tusked elephants with flint-tipped spears. They are also the most fundamental items of human adornment. Ostrich shell beads found in ancient cave deposits are considered among the earliest artistic expressions of humankind. Beads, it turns out, are as critical to the human identity as gold necklaces or lipstick.

In the meanwhile Atshumatso began setting off one group against another and fleecing the Dutch of funds that were given to him in order to obtain information as well as cattle. However, when the Cape smoke got in his eyes it would make him aggressive and he started having serious run-ins with his patrons. By and by the Dutch caught on, which led to his imprisonment, making him the first South African prisoner.

Conveniently there was an island just offshore, crowded with seals (robben) and penguins, that had already for a century or more served as a place of banishment for trouble causers, mainly miscreant sailors – mutineers, sodomites and the like. As a windswept place with no shelter, shade or even fresh water, it gained a reputation as a cruel place of exile. Sailors were known to take their own lives by jumping overboard rather than endure incarceration there.

Under Dutch control "the island" soon became a convenient place to stow rogues and rebels and basically throw away the keys: out of sight out of mind. An old myth is that no one ever escaped from the island, but almost from the start Atshumatso did, as did Krotoa later, and we'll get there in good time.

At one point the commander was informed that Atshumatso had fled into the interior. However, he and a small group were later found partying in the dunes near the mouth of the Salt River with the wine, bread and other food given to them for cattle bartering. That was only the beginning of the troubles between Dutch and Khoi and among the Khoi themselves over the favours and spoils of the Dutch (whom they found to be extremely naïve).

What particularly seems to have vexed the Protestant work ethic of the Europeans was that the Khoi did not fancy working for them. In one record we read that "the natives" (indigene) were too lazy to trouble themselves obtaining ivory, musk or feathers that would fetch high prices back in Europe.

Clearly it was not all shell collecting and braaivleis around the fort and things were destined to reach a flash point. The spark was ignited in 1658 when some Angolan slaves escaped from the fort and sought refuge with a Khoi clan. Among nomadic peoples the world over there is a code of protection for those seeking sanctuary. Bedouins, for example, will protect the life of a stranger in their care at all costs. The wilderness is unforgiving and next time it might be you. The early Europeans at the Cape would have had little regard for such cultural niceties.

Van Riebeeck ordered that three Khoi men be abducted and detained as a means of negotiating the return of the slaves. One Doman of the Goringhaiquas was so enraged by this that he began agitating towards conflict with the Dutch. Krotoa tried to persuade Doman that such a move would be foolish and would lead to his defeat. He in turn put the blame on her for all the trouble.

Through all this she kept up her Bible studies in the Castle chapel and in May of 1662 Krotoa was baptised as Eva (as in the first woman). She was the first indigenous person in South Africa to become a Christian.

Before the year was up there was another upheaval in her life when the Van Riebeecks departed to take up a more senior posting in Batavia and there was a new commander at the Cape, Zacharias Wagenear. On 22 November he wrote in his journal: "This morning we were told that our interpretess Krotoa of the Goringhaicona who had disappeared last Friday with both her children, without saying a word, was staying in the country with a freeman named Thielman Hendricx, whose house is situated right in the way leading to the aforesaid Hottentoos.

"This lewd vixen (die lichtvaerdige prije) has often played us this trick, throwing aside her clean and neat clothes, and instead, using stinking old cattle hides, just like all other dirty Hottentoo women do."

Two years later, in 1664, we find her not only back at the Castle but marrying a Danish surgeon stationed there, Pieter van Meerhoff, originally of Copenhagen. He would have been about twenty-seven at the time and she about twenty, but what to make of the two children mentioned earlier by Wagenear: who was their father? Had she been shacked up with Van Meerhoff for some years already, or were they perhaps the fruit of Jan van Riebeeck's lacivious loins, as has been suggested by some historical reconstructionists?

Virtually nothing is known about them other than we learn that, on marrying Eva (as she would have been to him), Van Meerhoff adopted a child named Jacob. It is possible the other two were also born out of wedlock because otherwise the dates do not tally.

The couple are recorded as having two children together, Pieternella and Salamon, before the family was posted to Robben Island, Pieter given the job of clearing the place of snakes, spiders and other vermin. There Krotoa became pregnant and in 1666 they returned to the mainland. It's possible the records have become confused and that Pieternella and Salamon were in fact the two children mentioned in 1662.

The good ship Van Meerhoff was sailing along happily enough, when suddenly it took a sharp turn to port. In February 1668 Pieter was aboard the *Westwout* on a slaving mission to the Indian Ocean when it anchored at Antogil Bay, Madagascar. He was killed there in a skirmish, but details are scarce.

Just how Krotoa took the news when eventually the *Westwout* returned to the Cape of Good Hope we do not know, but if she had once or twice before been an embarrassment to the genteel folk in the Castle, they hadn't seen anything yet. She took to the bottle in a crazed kind of way. Reports were that she became sexually depraved and returned to "native habits" (it's not clear whether or not these are meant to be the same thing).

Within in one year she became such an embarrassment "at the dinner table of Commander Wagenaer" that she was detained in the Castle. She managed to run away, leaving behind her children, but she was recaptured and banished to Robben Island. Her children were removed and put into foster care. She died on the island five years later, on 29 July 1674. She was around thirty or thirty-one.

However, even during her time on the island the feisty Khoi woman would not be forgotten. There was a small whaling or fishing settlement so hitching a ride back to the mainland would not have required any kind of Houdini act. Especially for a woman who we know was freer with her sexual favours than was held to be polite in "town".

Once back, Krotoa would pitch up, unannounced, at functions at the Castle, get roundly soaked and end up sleeping with whoever she fancied, or fancied her. Later she would be found sleeping in what I suppose you could call the street and promptly shipped back to the island. Repeat.

Sadly, even in death she was not left to the peace normally promised Christian souls. First she was buried on Robben Island. At some point her remains were moved to a grave next to the chapel inside the Castle, where she had been baptised twelve years previously. When that was demolished in 1700 her remains were reburied at the new Groote Kerk on the Heerengracht, at the bottom of the Company Gardens.

I was schooled under the harsh thumb of Christian National Education. Ours was a strict history told by the victors – the likes of Jan van Riebeeck, Simon van der Stel, Piet Retief, Paul Kruger, all white males. The Dutch, followed by the Trekboers, the Voortrekkers and then the emergent Afrikaners seemingly faced a lot of problems.

Our history text books, which we called Van Jaarsveld, were officially sanctioned by the Transvaal Education Department (TED/ TOD some might recall) and told us of the Hottentot problem, the Bushman problem, the Bantu problem and then the big one, the British problem. I was somewhat conflicted, given my partial British heritage. There is a saying that you make your own problems, but the full ramifications of this truism came to me only later.

In my dissenting student days I chose to do my final dissertation on the history of the black press in South Africa. In the process I came across an amazing book, *Time Longer Than Rope* by Eddie Roux, in the banned books section of the Rhodes University library. If the Rhodes Journalism Department was pink, the Wits University

Botany Department, where Roux spent most of his distinguished academic life, was not only a hotbed of green-fingered ecologists; it was positively scarlet with political activism.

The book opened my mind to an alternative politics of South Africa, one mainly of black males in powerful and assertive positions that challenged the political hegemony of the past three hundred years. Van Jaarsveld never mentioned the fact that heroic Governor Simon van der Stel was in fact of mixed race – anathema to the Afrikaner doctrine.

Suddenly it dawned on me that only white males were a part of our national narrative. There was an alternative parallel story of black males that was being told and written behind closed doors. The sub-title of Roux's book is "The Black Man's Struggle for Freedom in South Africa", but Eddie Roux's Wits of the 1930s, '40s and '50s was a different world to my Rhodes of the late 1970s-early-80s when women's liberation was marching alongside black political resistance. Where were the women in our history books?

For example, the freed slave most commonly known as Anna van Bengal who married the sergeant of the Castle during the term of Governor Simon van der Stel, the indefatigable Olof Bergh. When the governor died in 1712 Bergh bought his model farm Groot Constantia on auction. Turns out Bergh had been hoarding treasure from all the shipwrecks along the Cape coast he had sent out to investigate.

When Bergh died, Anna inherited South Africa's most iconic wine farm and in turn passed it on to her daughter and son-in-law. Anna made sure that not only she but also all her children and their children married well. Hers is now acknowledged as one of the longest and strongest Afrikaner dynasties. You wonder why Van Jaarsveld or any other mainstream historian never mentioned this remarkable woman or Krotoa … but then again, maybe not.

Atshumatso had featured – as Herry – in Van Jaarsveld's narrative as a troublesome Hottentot who the Dutch needed in order to conduct their business. I only became aware of the name Krotoa on my first visit to Robben Island after it had become a UNESCO World Heritage Site and place of political re-imagining. The guides on the island had been schooled in the alternative history and it was all so new and exciting to me that I set out to find more.

Comes the time comes the man – Mansell Upham in this case – the originator of the website and the Facebook page First Fifty Years, a project that digs into the documents of the early Cape settlement. Not everything that follows comes from this one source, but much of it does.

No sooner did I become interested in her story than I discovered Krotoa was hot political property. The crux of heated debates was that our history of that period was written by Europeans, more specifically men, with their very own peculiar views on matters religious, cultural and sexual, like having sex with slaves (men could, more or less openly, but women dare not: take heed Maria Mouton).

The spirit of Krotoa had remained quiet for some three hundred years until, seemingly out of the blue, a number of events intersected to resurrect her. In August 2016 a commemorative service was held by the Castle of Good Hope Control Board in her honour, with a memorial plaque unveiled by the Minister of Defence (the Castle has from day one been a military installation). Also around that time the Cape Town city council decided to rename a road after her, a lane really, running between Adderley and Burg streets.

Then, as if by cosmic synchronicity, word circulated that a movie about her would hit the big screens within the year. Even before it did, the debate started: would it be a romanticised post-colonial whitewash or would we be treated to a gritty depiction of the rough and complex life at the old Cape as it really might have been?

Wouldn't it be refreshing, someone posted on the e-grapevine, if the film was to tell the story of Krotoa from the Khoi point of view, showing what they made of the stuffy, avaricious, tactless Europeans? An advocate for Khoisan rights noted that the colonists held all the power when it came to writing history. "They depicted and demonised Krotoa as a drunkard, a whore and someone with loose morals."

An academic in the field of women and gender studies opined: "I can't prove that she was raped by Van Riebeeck himself, or by others. But if you look at her behaviour she exhibits signs of it. It's not a leap to imagine that she may have received alcohol instead of money as payment … She is the first abused woman who was forced into the tot system that became such a (sic) widespread." Not sound methodology, but yes, perhaps.

Unfortunately the film *Krotoa* did little to shine new light on the old story. When reviewing it the *Huffington Post* noted some critics claimed the film was a revival of the tired old gruel of European history. It quoted one mixed-race moviegoer saying: "I have never left a movie as upset as I did when I saw the *Krotoa* film recently."

My own issue with it was not so much the depictions of an unconvincing Commander Van Riebeeck raping his young charge, and she finding herself enjoying it, that so vexed some other people. I found the lack of any redeeming artistic merit too embarrassing to endure for more than half an hour.

I walked out the Labia Theatre into a balmy Cape summer evening. As I made my way past the Company Gardens I imagined the ghost of Krotoa walking in the crepuscular half-light of Upper Orange Street. It's one of the preferred hangouts of the Bergies, the perpetually homeless descendants of the Khoi people who seem to fade away with the dawn and emerge at night to prowl a parallel universe, moving about in the shadows unseen by the greater part of a society to which they have never belonged.

I could sense, feel, that what a member of the Castle Control Board had said at Krotoa's memorial service went to the heart of her story: that "although she was a tragic character she did survive being treated in a sub-humane manner. I think she died of a broken heart."

Who is Dawid Stuurman and Why Do They Want to Name a Road After Him?[1]

What's in a name, anyway?

One of the great – if not the greatest – myths of old South African history is that white settlers moving inexorably eastwards first came into contact with black people moving south on the banks of the Great Fish River. The historical reality is that explorers and later Trekboers met black pastoralists up the Long Kloof (possibly as far as present-day Oudtshoorn) as well as around Storms River – the western extent of good grazing for their cattle. The eastern grasslands proved addictive to the Boers whose cattle had been raised on a coarse diet of fynbos.

One of the more grotesque laws – if not the most – passed by the white South African government was the Native Land Act of 1913,

---

1 A play on the title of one of my favourite '70s movies *Who Is Harry Kellerman And Why Is He Saying All Those Terrible Things About Me*, starring Dustin Hoffman

which forbade anyone deemed to be not white from owning land in the land of their birth, the land of their ancestors going back hundreds and thousands of years. This story is mostly about land, more to the point, land grabs. In the bigger canvas of political unfolding no group was treated more shabbily than the Khoisan, or Khoi, the brown-skinned herders who the Dutch called Hottentots.

As I write this story, in mid-2018, there is a lot of hullabaloo about land issues, as well as the renaming of places and streets. Happily Cape Town has so far been spared some of the overzealous excesses of the Durban city management: to wit Dr Langalibalele Dube Street, or Griffiths Mxenge/Mangosuthu Highway. There are also Samora Machel, Kenneth Kaunda and Che Guevara streets – people with absolutely no connection to Durban.

"They've swapped our heroes for their heroes!" one irate letter writer grumbled in the press. That's how it rolls: to the victor the spoils, but, to be fair, there are also Helen Joseph, David Webster, Alan Paton and Henry Pennington among the new street names to be found at eThekwini.

In my neck of the woods, along the more famous Nelson Mandela and Helen Suzman boulevards, we have Landsdowne renamed Imam Abdullah Haron Road. He was the first coloured political campaigner in the Cape to die in police detention. Also, the arbitrarily named Concert Boulevard in Retreat which is now Joe Marks Boulevard (others in that suburb include fatuous Choir, Solo, Trumpet and Sonata streets). Joe, the son of a fisherman, was a vegetable seller and construction worker who joined Umkhonto we Sizwe and was a champion of community issues in the Cape Flats.

What is not always appreciated by the naysayers is that, by far, the majority of these name changes – whether in Cape Town, Durban, Johannesburg or elsewhere – honour local people, many of whom gave their lives in the struggle for political and land rights. How bad can that be?

On our council table, as I write this, is the renaming of Baden Powell Drive, that lovely stretch of blacktop that curves all the way along False Bay from Muizenberg to Macassar. Colonel, later Lieutenant-General Lord Robert Stephenson Smyth Baden Powell was the British defender of Mafeking (Mahikeng) during the Anglo-Boer War siege. Baden Powell was a Charterhouse and India man through and through. The boy scouts movement he started was based on his experiences using boys as messengers during the siege. One of their duties was to deliver "tea" each afternoon to households in town in order to keep up morale. It was in fact a hot drink called Chervil and it was made from the boiled down remains of horses, mules and donkeys. Once the war was concluded, Baden Powell headed straight back to Blighty, wrote a book about and began giving lectures on the art of scouting based on his South African experiences. They proved so popular that the Scouts movement sprang from them. Its origins were African but just about everything else about it was Anglo-Indian: all that wolf pack, dib-dib, arkela stuff.

The new name proposed for Baden Powell Drive is Dawid Stuurman. Most (white) South Africans will not have heard of him and will presume it is just another poke in the political eye, but perhaps not. Allow me to elucidate and then you can decide …

It's the year 1806. Ink on the Treaty of Amiens between Great Britain and the French Republic has only just dried and already the French have started rattling their sabres again (things at the old Cape always hinged on larger events in Europe). Britain has taken the Cape from the short-lived Batavian Republic in order to poke a cannon or two at Bonaparte's ambitions in the Indian Ocean.

What is not always appreciated is that the British were generally against expending much-needed resources, keeping a small, costly and troublesome colony at the Cape. Prime Minster Pitt and Lord of the Admiralty Horatio Nelson were dead against having even a toehold at the foot of Africa. Their solution was to dispatch some of the duller military types and less luminescent administrators to our shores, more the pity for us. However, as so often happens, these "little men" had ambitions way beyond their capabilities.

New governor, Sir David Baird, dispatched a small force under the command of General Barrow from Cape Town to hold down the Eastern Cape. As with the Dutch before them, the official British policy was to re-affirm native land tenure and disarm the Boer expansionists from any further acts of aggression or expansion into the disputed Zuurveld region. However, things did not work out quite as intended.

No sooner had General Barrow led his column out of Fort Frederick at Algoa Bay on his first reconnaissance of his new domain, than they were approached by a group of Khoi "outlandishly dressed in the oddments of European clothing that they had adopted together with their traditional sheepskins".

The general had no idea what to make of them, nor their demand that the British help to restore their independence from the "calamities and sufferings under the yoke of the Boers". "We have yet a great deal of our blood to avenge" their leader, who identified himself as Klaas Stuurman, told the uncomfortable officer.

As a teenager, Klaas's brother Dawid had been forced to work on a Boer farm in the Gamtoos River valley. Among many incidents of mistreatment by white farmers of their Khoi-San labourers reported to the missionaries at Bethalsdorp was of Dawid Stuurman being "flogged on the wheel" by the Vermaaks, salt rubbed into his wounds and being left to blister in the summer sun.

It was hardly surprising, therefore, when the Second Frontier War (1779–1783) broke out, the Stuurmans, together with a number of other Khoi people, absconded from the Gamtoos and fled eastwards. Armed conflict between white settlers and Khoi pastoralists had been an on-off affair for some time.

The Khoi stronghold was the Bruintjieshoogte, the area around Graaff-Reinet, including the high ground of the Stormberg to the north. They had been at odds with the Trekboers since the latter absconded from control of the Castle. In time Klaas Stuurman became their leader, or captain.

At first the British tended to side with the Xhosa and the Khoi, finding the Boers to be duplicitous and even treacherous. It was callous men such as the Prinsloos, Bezuidenhouts and De Buys who kept on pushing the colonial boundary ever eastwards, past the Sundays, then the Bushmans, the Great Fish, the Keiskamma and eventually all the way to the Kei River. In retaliation, Stuurman's people burned their homesteads and stole their cattle.

Unfortunately, for just about everyone, the man the British

appointed as drostdy (magistrate) of the Eastern Frontier was Jacob Cuyler, a man "devoid of any Enlightenment-inspired sentiment and idealism, who acted with arrogant displeasure and vindictive fury to anyone who dared to oppose his will and commands". He was given a colonelship and carte blanche in the affairs of his new realm.

In fact, Cuyler was an American, a British loyalist from Albany in New York. When England lost the American War of Independence and their richest colony, Cuyler fled to the Cape. The Albany district, the land between the Sundays and Great Fish rivers (also known as the Zuurveld), was named by him in remembrance of his old, forfeited homeland.

He was expected to keep peace between the Boer, Xhosa and Khoi but from the get-go, in just about everything he did and said, he sided with the white settlers. In his haste and recklessness he destroyed any vestiges of goodwill between the various parties, broke treaties and rescinded land grants to Xhosas and Khoi. Of all the misguided and mistrusted figures of this time and place, for sheer bombast and deceit, Cuyler is matched only by Harry Smith.

While the Trekboers on the Eastern Frontier continued the old game under Dutch rule of grabbing land and press-ganging the Khoi into forced labour, the British introduced a "pass law". They did it on what they thought were humanitarian grounds, to ensure fair pay and some protection from mistreatment, but it was the beginning of one of the most heinous mechanisms of racial control introduced in South Africa.

Klaas Stuurman and his people, far from having the British as a new ally, found themselves pitted against both Boer and Brit. The land that had been granted them around the Bethelsdorp mission and along the Gamtoos River was hemmed in by Cuyler in every way possible. When Klaas died in a hunting incident in 1809 his brother, Dawid, took over as captain of the last group of Khoi with freehold title in the Eastern Cape. No sooner had he stepped up than Dawid found himself in conflict with Cuyler.

Cuyler feared these land rights gave the Khoi an opportunity to forge tighter bonds with the Xhosa. He was easily persuaded by the Boers that this was a very bad thing. When in early 1809 Stuurman resisted an attempt by a commando to seize two of his people who had fled from forced labour on Boer farms and sought refuge at the Gamtoos settlement, Cuyler grabbed the opportunity.

Aware of Stuurman's power and temper, he wove a web of deceit. He sweet-talked a Boer friend of Stuurman's into summoning the Khoi leader to his home to talk things over. When Stuurman arrived he was set upon by a posse and dispatched to Cape Town in irons with three others.

Those of his people who did not manage to escape into the fastness of the Bruintjieshoogte or further into the welcome arms of the Xhosa (they were as expert marksmen as were the Boers) were captured and distributed as servants and labourers among Boer farms. Meanwhile, the four captives in Cape Town were convicted of "disobedience to the field cornet" and in September sentenced to life terms of hard labour on Robben Island.

In December, Stuurman and the other three managed to escape from the island by taking a whaling boat and rowing to the mainland. The others were recaptured, but Stuurman managed to make his way back to the Eastern Cape.

During the Fifth Frontier War of 1818–1819 he sided with the Xhosa and was captured along with the prophet-warrior Makana (Makhanda). With him and some other Xhosa leaders, Stuurman was sent back to Robben Island. There he remained until August of 1820, when again he managed to escape during a prison mutiny.

For a third time Stuurman was captured, this time as he stepped ashore Bloubergstrand; Makana drowned while trying to steady the rowing boat in the churning surf. Stuurman was again tried and as a two-time escapee from Robben Island he was sentenced to life imprisonment at the penal settlement of New South Wales. On 16 December 1820 he was back on the island, where he was kept chained awaiting transportation.

In April 1823, the convict ship *Brampton* reached Sydney with Stuurman among a group of eleven South African convicts. After labouring for six years as a criminal he was given a ticket of leave, which allowed him to work for wages. David Stuurman died on 22 February 1830 and was buried at the Devonshire Cemetery. Today the Central Sydney Railway Station stands on the site.

I first sniffed the trail of Dawid Stuurman while researching the history of street names of Cape Town. Some people collect train engine numbers, others antique clocks. I knew a guy who collected old ammunition casings. We kind of sniggered about it but his collection sold for a small fortune. For me, it was street names. When a magazine publisher I know found out about my unusual interest he asked me to write a series of articles on the street names of the major cities in South Africa.

It's amazing what the fabric weaved by the warp and weft of street names tells you about the history of a place. My first job was in the Johannesburg town planning department. There I learned about the two surveyors tasked with laying out the road network of Randjieslaagte gold-rush camp, what is now the CBD. They started at the eastern end and named it Nugget Street. From there they worked their ways westwards, one at the north end and the other at the south.

Where they met, at Bree Street, they found there was a discrepancy in their measurements. It turned out one had been using English feet and the other Cape feet, which are not the same. Instead of re-measuring the whole thing, they simply put a kink in each north-south running street where they crossed Bree. That is why today you'll find the streets running north-south have an increasingly large kink as you move westwards across the city. That might have been the spark.

If it were put to the vote, I know next to whose name I would put my 'X' for that lovely curve of road that runs around the fairest of bays, bowled in along its eastern margin by the pleated curtain of the Hottentots-Holland or "home of the Hottentots" mountains. What about you?

Claude Finch-Davies –
Fallen Bird Man

The artist who flew too close to the sun

THE STORY OF FINCH-DAVIES HAS been written several times before, once in a book and also a few times in specialist media. The prevalent story about the bird artist who was a South African Icarus is material enough, but that would be only half the real and full story.

In all works of tragedy the Greeks taught us that the central character needs to have a basic flaw. Seemingly small enough at first, but then the gods start picking at it like a scab they cannot resist. "Like wanton boys to flies are we to the gods," cries Shakespeare's King Lear, "they kill us for their sport."

Any fly, frog or grasshopper will do as well, but the gods seem to take greatest pleasure in choosing those who seem destined to be faster, higher or stronger, building them up only to tear them down. Flood their lives with sunshine and good fortune before they pee down on their parade.

One more thing needs to be put in place before a full-scale drama can unfold: the tragic hero must be given the means and opportunity to commit a moral crime. Like when the King of Scotland comes visiting Macbeth's castle just when Lady Macbeth is at her craziest and infects her nobleman husband's ambitions with murderous bile, or Icarus flying too close to the sun on his wax-glued wings, trying to reach the realm of the gods, only to have them melt and to fall from the sky and from grace. Such was the fate of Finch-Davies, South Africa's own Icarus.

Claude Gibney Davies (he pronounced it Davis) was born in Delhi in 1875, son of a major-general and a naturalist artist mother (she was reputed to be an expert on Indian snakes). His mother taught him to do watercolours, but that talent was soon put on a back burner. The lad was shipped off to England for schooling where he did not excel. By fudging his age he managed to enlist in the Cape Mounted Rifles and arrived on the toe of Table Mountain in 1893 at the age of eighteen.

From there, until he was shipped off to German South West Africa at the outbreak of war in 1914, he spent almost all his time on patrol in the bush. From notes on his paintings we read about his adventures in Puffadder Bush, N'gosa Bush, Barolo Bush, Imboitzi, Umzinvumba, Umzinkaba and many other bushy spots in Pondoland and East Griqualand. There were also excursions elsewhere, such as a stint at Kuruman and along the border of Bechuanaland.

The young soldier seems to have been more than happy roughing it in Africa and steadily he rose through the ranks. By the close of the Anglo-Boer War in 1902 he held the rank of sergeant. Although he started making notes on his bird observations from around 1898, his first known painting (not a very good one by all accounts) was made only in 1903. It was of an Ethiopian snipe he'd shot near Lusikisiki. But the quality of his paintings improved rapidly.

He seems to have spent most of his time out shooting, either for specimens to study and paint or for the pot. One aspect of his work is notable from the first, that each painting is annotated with his observations on locality, behaviour, colour and other attributes. Remember that the avian life of the region was still little known and so these would, in time and as his status and self-assuredness grew, become important ornithological references.

He shot a Namaqua dove on the school grounds in Flagstaff, along with several other species for study purposes. Red-capped larks were common on the parade ground at Lusikisiki, he notes. Bitterns were "not bad eating", yellow-billed ducks "good sporting birds and excellent eating" and hadedas "most excellent for eating" (who would have thought!).

Shoot as he did, in the custom of the day, Davies was generally and genuinely fond of birds. He nursed and kept many as pets, including a white-necked raven and two spur-wing geese. Also in the custom of the day he seems to have had a Mpondo woman look after him and he often gives the Xhosa name for the birds he painted.

Davies often had trouble identifying the birds he collected, owing to the poor references then available. Layard and Sharpe's *Birds of South Africa* was at the time an inadequate standard reference.

Davies did all his work in exactly the same brand of sketchbooks, consisting of forty sheets each, with canvas cover and leather carrying strap (they cost one shilling each). He filled thirty of these books with more than a thousand paintings in all, most of them with accompanying field notes.

In the beginning he leant on an H Langton, clearly another bird enthusiast who assisted with bird identification and information, but Davies was on the up and up as a birder and soon we hear of him making contact with some of the leading birders of the day. He reputedly had excellent eyesight, which aided him tremendously in his fieldwork.

In 1907 we find his first published work, 'Notes on birds observed and collected in the Districts of Port St Johns, Lusikisiki, Flagstaff, Bizana and Pondoland' in the *Journal of the South African Ornithologist's Union*. He followed this the next year with 'Some notes on the wildfowl and waterbirds of Matatiele, East Griqualand'.

By this time he was sending skins of interesting birds he collected to Alwin Haagner, president of the South African Ornithological Union, for identification. More papers followed on his bird observations. In 1910 he published a paper discussing the plumage variations of the mountain chat. By this time he was being recognised as a reliable bird illustrator.

In 1911 the Transvaal Museum printed three of his plates, featuring six species that were described by Haagner. When World War I broke out in 1914 Davies's regiment was sent to German South West Africa and so he began his paintings and papers on birds of that arid region. That year also marked his first correspondence with Austin Roberts, assistant head of the Department of Higher Vertebrates at the Transvaal Museum and a noted bird expert. He would later become head of that department.

The medical officer of Davies's regiment, The First South African Rifles, was LC Thompson and they, together with the doctor's wife, enjoyed weekend excursions into the bush to go birding. Mrs Thompson would accompany them, skin their birds and provide endless cups of tea. The enlisted man also had the opportunity of borrowing the good doctor's binoculars, the privilege of officers.

Sergeant Davies seemed to show scant regard for physical discomfort on campaign. He would wander off into the veld, his tunic pockets stuffed with brushes and paints, and often return with birds in his pockets wrapped in paper. At times he would sketch them roughly in the field and then cut off the legs to keep for detailed work back at camp.

After the war, when Major Boyd Horsbrugh began his monograph on game birds and waterfowl of South Africa, he asked Thompson if there was anyone back in South Africa who might be able to illustrate it, although he held out little hope. The doctor was well acquainted with Davies's work and had no hesitation in recommending the sergeant of the Rifle Brigade.

Davies produced ninety-six illustrations for Horsbrugh's book, as well supplying notes of his own for which the major credited him and paid him handsomely. This project was the game changer in the soldier-birder-painter's life. The money would come in handy to augment his meagre military salary when, while on sick leave in the Cape, he met and (probably emboldened by his new status as a published illustrator) soon became engaged to Miss Aileen Finch. She was the daughter of a Captain Finch, head of the RSPCA in Cape Town.

Although his first brush with fame was with game and water birds, his real passion was for raptors. In 1911 he had commenced his twentieth sketch book, this and several subsequent ones being devoted to eagles, owls, hawks and falcons. By and by he also filled three sketchbooks with paintings of Indian game birds (using borrowed skins and illustrations), but these were lost while on loan to Alwin Haagner. At the time of his death he was about to commence on a monograph of sunbirds.

Davies was seen causing waves for the first time in 1913 when he wrote to the *South African Journal* that a falcon (*Falco horsbrughi*) described by Gunning and Roberts in 1911 as a new species was in fact merely the immature form of the red-necked falcon, *Falco ruficollis*. Not everyone was thrilled with the demotion (Austin Roberts clearly did not agree with Davies and in the 1940 first edition of his own *Birds of South Africa* he included the red-necked falcon *Chiquera ruficollis daviesii* as well as Horsbrugh's falcon, *Chiquera horsbrughi*. This was corrected in the third edition in 1970 showing, as Davies had argued, that *horsbrughi* was merely the immature form of *ruficollis*, which we now know as *Falco chiquera*.)

Davies worked swiftly, and his drawing was extremely accurate. When brought a specimen he would quickly capture the colour of the eyes, bill and legs, as there was little time to paint the entire specimen. Back in his tent he would colour in the rest of the image. For the fine details of the eyes and leg scales he used brushes with just a few bristles each.

He experimented with active poses but soon settled on static, classic stances, seeing his work not as art but merely as an accurate recording of bird form and colour. His main focus was on the study of birds and his paintings were study aids.

Davies did not produce much work during the second half of the Great War, although he was still borrowing study skins from the Transvaal Museum as well as issues of *The Ibis*, the journal of the British Ornithologist's Union, from his pen pal and fellow bird scholar Austin Roberts. *The Ibis* contained plates by many of Europe's leading bird artists.

In 1916, with wedding plans being made, Davies had his first material squabble with Roberts. It was over the price of bird skins the soldier had provided to the museum in Pretoria. In spite of their ornithological disagreements, correspondence between the two men proceeded in the formal and courteous style of the time.

In August of that year Lieutenant Davies married Aileen Finch, her father insisting the couple take the name Finch-Davies. The newly promoted officer's peers found it most amusing. But things seemed to have progressed somewhat less cordially in the Finch-Davies marriage. Apparently the good wife had no idea just how fixated her husband was in his pursuit of birds. She nagged him, complained when he went off birding and is said to even have torn up some of his paintings.

Be that as it may, their first child, William, was born in Windhoek in August of 1917. On the birding side things were flying happily along. His personal copy of Horsbrugh's book overflowed with annotations as well as sketches and paintings of a newly discovered species of francolin, both male and female plumages. Furthermore, his old mentor Alwin Haagner presented him with a signed copy of his *Sketches of S. African Bird Life*.

Following the end of the Great War in 1918, Davies's 'On birds collected and observed in the districts of Okanjande and Outjo, S. W. African Protectorate' was printed in the first volume of the *South African Journal of Natural History*. He also became a founder member of the new South African Biological Society.

Later that year, however, Finch-Davies once again let slip his frustrations of feeling isolated from the centres of birding knowledge. He wrote to the director of the Transvaal Museum, complaining that he had been hurt by the treatment served to him by Austin Roberts, having repeatedly written to him but receiving no reply. The fact was that the soldier now had no war to fight and time on his hands, whereas the museum man had a real job and was very often away on field trips dealing with outbreaks of dread diseases and the like.

In response, Roberts told his superior that Finch-Davies was wont to complain and pester him. However, not long after this niggardly interchange Finch-Davies was transferred to Roberts Heights in Pretoria, the theatre of his downfall just as a second child, Bethea Alice, was being readied to make her worldly entrance.

The artist seems to have spent much, if not most, of his free time in Pretoria in the archives of the Transvaal Museum, although documentation is scarce owing to that most wondrous of modern inventions, the telephone.

The letters might have become infrequent but our man was writing aplenty. First an article in *The Ibis* arguing that the raptor described by Gurney as *Hieraaëtus ayresi* was in fact (and once again) merely the immature form of the bird Sharpe had designated *Lophotriochis lucani*. Roberts called it *Anamalaetus dubius* (note that species name), which today we know as *Aquila ayresii*, the Ayres's hawk-eagle. Given what trouble the experts had, it's little wonder new birders find the raptors nearly as hard to distinguish as they do the LBJs.

Then came his big paper, 'Notes on South African Accipitres' which outlined the biology and behaviour of all the birds of prey of the region. It was the first accurate and comprehensive work on the group and brought Finch-Davies into the inner sanctum of southern African ornithology. The bird artist was now reaching for the stars and ready for the plucking.

In January 1920 Dr Breijer, director of the Transvaal Museum, wrote to the Secretary of the Interior that Mr Austin Roberts in the Department of the Higher Vertebrates had discovered a number of colour plates missing from various reference books in their collection. That was the beginning of the meltdown; our Icarus was nearing the sun.

The Commissioner of Police was alerted and the CID called in to investigate. Their initial investigation showed up thirty-seven missing plates. In time the number would climb to more than two hundred. A trap was laid and who walked in but Claude Gibney Finch-Davies, bird artist and authority of repute.

In the conventional mythology of this story we see Austin Roberts working with the CID to gather evidence and lay the trap, but, as we shall see, while the first part of that statement is true the second is the diametric opposite of the facts.

Either way, by mid-January 1920, Lieutenant Finch-Davies was under arrest while a thorough search of his own premises was conducted. Two hundred and thirty stolen plates were inventoried although the accused argued that some, if not many, of them came from his own copies of the various publications.

On 30 January Finch Davies wrote to the museum director, offering some explanation and begging mercy: "Perhaps you once entertained some liking and respect for me, and that perhaps you would see me and hear anything I might say in excuse for my behaviour. God knows that after all the kindness you have shown me, it must appear to you that I cannot have any excuse for what I have done, and now I have come to realise it. I cannot understand myself how I could have behaved as I have. I can only think that I must have suffered from the madness of the collector, which distorts the moral sense."

He begs forgiveness, noting that he is forty-six years old, just three years short of being pensioned off and he has two children with a third on its way. His wife would be the real victim if he were to find himself severely punished, and so on.

"I have, I believe, been able to do something towards the cause of Science, both by my studies and by my paintings of South African birds. I have always been particularly fond of ornithology, and have done my best to further the knowledge of this subject, and had hopes of continuing to do so."

He offered to hand over to the museum his entire collection of paintings in "part repayment" for his crime and to repay the museum all its costs in replacing the damaged publications. During the exchange of correspondence over these matters, the museum valued the Finch-Davies collection at £200 while the replacement cost to the museum was fixed at £380.

On 18 March Finch-Davies was charged, brought before the army inspector-general, "severely reprimanded" and transferred to the Castle in Cape Town to serve in a menial clerical position. His old friend Alwin Haagner, by then director of the National Zoological Gardens, interceded on his behalf and convinced his commanding officer (a friend) not to court martial the fallen soldier, the birdman who had flown so high only to crash back down to earth. Aileen remained behind in Pretoria to give birth to their third child, Hugh Claude.

On 9 August 1920 the Cape Town obituaries included an entry

entitled 'Gifted Painter's End. Sudden Death At Castle'. His death certificate gave the cause of death being angina pectoris, a heart attack. And yet the previous day had been spent in the company of his family, and his wife reported he had been "in the best of health".

Aileen packed all their belongings, and in September she and the three children boarded the *Balmoral Castle* bound for England, and that is where she died, by all accounts in poverty.

Thus ends the orthodox version of the story of Claude Gibney Finch-Davies, the one that is generally known to those with an interest in things birds and birding, even if it leaves an undertone of suspicion over the real cause of death.

Close reading of the most comprehensive biography of Finch-Davies, written by Dr Alan Kemp and published by the Transvaal Museum in 1976, is telling. Kemp had stepped up to fill the shoes of Roberts's successor, OPM Prozesky, as the keeper of the birds in 1970. It turns out Roberts refused to play any part in the trapping or prosecution of Finch-Davies, his close friend.

While much has been made of the squabbles between Roberts and Finch-Davies and raised to conflict level in some versions, the opposite is the reality. It's true it was not all hugs and kisses between the two men, and Finch-Davies is more than once shown to be a prickly character, but that did not seem to puncture their relationship.

On 23 June Roberts wrote: "I am glad to hear that you are not antagonistic to me, though your letters certainly leave that impression. I have already had to put up with so much opposition from quarters where one would expect to receive assistance, that I am getting accustomed to it. It seems to be an unfortunate fact that in scientific matters in which workers are professionally brothers, one meets anything but fellowship."

Alwin Haagner is also revealed to have been a true friend of the artist, not only in helping to arrange for Davies to be published in the South African Ornithological Union's journal, but also interceding on his behalf when he was arrested. Without Haagner's input Finch-Davies almost certainly would have been court martialed and faced severe penalty.

Furthermore, Austin Roberts refused to make an affidavit to the

CID against the stricken man. He wrote to his superiors: "I did not feel disposed to do so, the evidence available being insufficient and because I could not conceive it possible that Finch-Davies would have done it."

And so things might have remained in the public mind (as well as my own) had it not been for a document I chanced upon one day in Chancellor Oppenheimer Library at the University of Cape Town. I photocopied a section of an article entitled 'Austin Roberts and the Finch-Davies Tragedy'. I tucked it into my copy of the Finch-Davies biography and forgot it there for more than nearly 30 years.

When recently I opened the book it dropped out, but stupid me, I had neglected to note the details of the publication and so to this day have no clue as to its provenance. I have searched high and low to no avail.

The first myth it shoots out the sky is the oft-repeated fiction in the story of Finch-Davies of casting Roberts as the bad guy. The photocopied text reveals that the correspondence (which starts mid-1913) between Finch Davies in the veld and Roberts in the town was positively copious. In 1917 alone, when the soldier was billeted in Windhoek, twenty-three letters are known to have been exchanged.

Quite early on Roberts asked Finch-Davies to address his letters to the museum man's private home: "They are rather inquisitive at the office. The subject of birds is more than mere employment."

The next revelation is on the matter of Finch-Davies's death. Already Alan Kemp had raised the possibility of suicide in his biography, alluding to an overdose of morphine, but adding "there is no evidence to support this idea". However, it was clearly a case of smoke having been detected in his room at the Castle. Now comes a new petard to hoist our character even closer to the sun's withering glow.

My photocopy refers to information contained in the *History of the South African Museum 1825–1975* by Roger Summers: "In 1920 there occurred a strange and disturbing episode" (in the saga of Finch-Davies).

A Dr AW Rogers, who had previously worked at the national

museum in Cape Town, was transferred to Pretoria where, apparently, he learned about the saga of the disappearing bird illustrations and subsequent events. Rogers wrote to his old colleagues in Cape Town. He warned them the culprit, since apprehended, had been transferred to Cape Town and that they should be on their guard for any similar such pilfering.

By the time they received this warning the looting had already begun. It was noted by the director there, Dr L Péringuey, that, in particular, issues of the British Museum catalogues of birds appeared to have been mutilated.

"The suspect, who is well known in his field of study, and had been allowed the run of the library, was asked to call on the director, but the day before the interview took place he shot himself. His guilt was subsequently proved but none of the missing plates was ever recovered."

So now we have not only a recidivistic thief but also death by heart attack, a morphine overdose as well as by shooting. The national museum found a hundred and thirty-two plates missing from their collection. It is not beyond imagination that the condemned man had taken the plates from the Cape Town museum in the hope of passing them off as his own property in order to repay what he owned to the Transvaal Museum. Or simply that he could not tame the madness.

Concerned by the plight of Aileen and the children back in Pretoria, Austin Roberts looked deeper into the value of the Finch-Davies collection in his care. It transpired that in order to give the paintings a valuation, Haagner likely looked only at the first sketchbook. When Roberts more carefully assessed the entire set he came to a conservative estimated value of £1,250.

Roberts wrote to his boss, saying the museum had suffered damages that could be valued at no more than £400. He then urged the director, Breijer, to make good to Finch-Davies's widow the difference. The matter went to the museum committee, but in spite of urging, they did – or decided to do – nothing to make amends.

Roberts did manage to sell, on behalf of the widow, two paintings that remained in her possession. The buyer was the dead man's former friend in the military, Major Thompson, for £7.7/-. That was the only money Aileen Finch-Davies ever received from her husband's work. She probably regretted tearing up those earlier paintings.

In the final sentence of his letter to the director, Roberts urges: "The paintings are far too good to be wasted by lying in obscurity." This revelation ushers in the final chapter of this byzantine chronicle.

Throughout the 1930s Austin Roberts was extremely busy working on his own definitive work on birds, which he planned to title *A Handbook of South African Birds*. All this time the Finch-Davies collection lay in their canvas covers inside an orange metal trunk that was locked in one of the Transvaal Museum's storerooms. Having seen and appreciated the quality of the paintings, as well as their almost comprehensive coverage of the region's species, it is likely Roberts looked forward to using them in his future book.

That was not to be. Lawyers informed the museum that, if they wished to avoid any resulting payments, they should not make any use of the paintings for at least fifty years after the death of the artist – the standard time at which copyright for creative work lapses.

This caused a big problem for Roberts – and future expenses far greater than any that might have otherwise been incurred – for now he had to find someone who could complete something like a thousand illustrations of the highest artistic standard, while at the same time being scientifically accurate.

This is the point where Norman KC Lighton, architectural draughtsman for the Public Works Department in Pretoria, walks onto our stage. From the age of around six, Lighton had begun drawing animals he found in the veld around the family's smallholding north of Pretoria where he had been born in 1904. While at school, his parents allowed him to take private art lessons.

Working for the Public Works Department, Lighton often used his lunch hours to paint animals in the Transvaal Museum collection. This led to a small commission from museum director Breijer to paint identification plates for the museum's bird collection, which, presumably, is where he would have met Roberts.

Lighton was duly seconded from Public Works to the museum where he worked under the direction of Roberts, but there was a condition: Public Works was to be compensated to pay for Lighton's replacement. This was agreed to because the South African Bird Book Fund had been created by a group of bird-minded businessmen including CJ Swierstra (who succeeded Breijer as director of the Transvaal Museum), CS "Punch" Barlow and AV Lindberg, chairman of the Central News Agency or CNA. They raised £1,256 to cover the costs of producing Roberts's book.

The problem was that the size of the task given to Lighton was greater than anyone, he in particular, could have imagined. By the time the book was ready to go to print World War II had flared up and all the trust money had been used up paying for Lighton's time.

The stress of getting the book into print caused great anxiety for both writer and artist. Roberts suffered from chronic hyperacidity and developed duodenal ulcers. Lighton, who had to put in more than a thousand hours' unpaid overtime in order to complete his fifty-six colour plates, suffered a loss of eyesight. Fortunately this proved to be only a temporary condition.

With the publishing war chest exhausted, Lindberg and the CNA stepped in and offered to pay the printers in London for two thousand two hundred copies. They cleared customs in Cape Town in July 1940 (lucky for them the cargo ship was not sunk by German U-boats that were at the time active around the South African coast) and went on sale at the cost of thirty shillings each. Roberts and Lighton were each presented with one free leather-bound copy.

I first became interested in birds on a trip with some teenage friends to the Okavango Delta in the mid-1970s. I could not believe the world could contain so many birds and for my next birthday asked for the current version of Roberts and a pair of binoculars. They became my constant companions on many adventures over the years.

In the early 1980s I visited the Transvaal Museum in Pretoria, while researching my first book on mountains. In the small shop a set of bird prints caught my eye and I duly coughed up the asking price of R70. Collector's madness if you like, for I was of frugal means.

While poring over my third edition of Roberts (I now have all seven), I became aware of a similarity between some of the paintings in that book credited to N Lighton and my Finch-Davies prints. Close comparison showed they were very close copies of the old soldier's work.

Meanwhile, Alan Kemp had retrieved the Finch-Davies paintings from their vault and arranged for Johannesburg publisher of fine books, Guy Winchester-Gould, to reissue them in several volumes. I bought those I could, which included a facsimile edition of Horsbrugh's book on game birds, also published by Winchester Press. Only the *Birds of Prey*, published as a small collector's edition, remained elusive.

However, I did finally track down a block (an unbound proof copy) on the shelves at Winchester Press while they were being cleared on the closure of the business. My block was sent to master binder Peter Carstens, who had bound the original edition, and it became the pride of my book collection.

It then became clear to me that Lighton had copied many of the Finch-Davies paintings down to the stone or branch perches (he sometimes transposed the images, as in the case of the male and female bateleurs). This certainly seemed to fit the canonical version of the story wherein Roberts, with Lighton a willing accomplice, conspired to defraud the original artist of his copyright and reputation.

However, it all became clear when I studied my photocopied manuscript. What really transpired was that Roberts had given Lighton the Finch-Davies works as references. When the Public Works man found himself with his back to the deadline wall, his life in tatters, his finances at risk and his health fading, he did what any reasonable man would have done in order to fulfill his contract. He copied them.

That first edition of *The Birds of South Africa* sold out in six weeks and it went on to enjoy nine impressions between 1940 and 1957. To date there have been six fully revised editions which have sold more than three hundred thousand copies – the biggest selling non-fiction book in South African publishing history.

Apart from their free copies, the two authors did not receive one penny or cent in royalties from the book.

Maria Mouton – Burn the Witch

How a colonial woman and her two slave accomplices were tortured in the Castle of Good Hope

How **often have you read** a short news snippet in a newspaper or magazine and thought, wow, there must be one heck of a back story there to uncover? 'Man shoots family with crossbow', or 'Body found on Wild Coast with bag of diamonds in coat pocket'. Maybe it's because I was trained as a journalist to have a nose for a story, but at times like these I find myself concocting accounts about what might have been.

In 1999 I found myself collaborating with historian Nigel Penn to produce a series of magazine features to commemorate the centenary of the start of the Anglo-Boer War. That was also the year his enthralling book on the eighteenth Century at the Cape, *Rogues, Rebels and Runaways*, was published.

Among the fantastical tales of serially adulterous beer brewers, runaway slaves and rebellious burghers was a short insert, just one paragraph, about a woman, Maria Mouton, who was executed for murder, along with her slave lover and his accomplice. That paragraph, more than anything else in a book packed with incredible events and remarkable characters, had me hankering for more information.

By following Nigel's footnotes back into dank and musty archival pasts, I found a story far more complete and lurid than any I might have conjured in my limited mind. The Protestant Dutch in South Africa were much more interested in matters of the flesh and the purse than the spirit, quite unlike their Spanish Catholic counterparts in South America. Their reasons for squashing serious breaches of the social code were based on the need for commerce to continue unchallenged. However, their brutal and bloodthirsty methods equaled anything the deranged Inquisition dreamed up. Coincidentally, this story is rooted in the religious conflicts of the time.

The Mouton family hailed from Flanders. Maria's mother had died in childbirth and in due course her father remarried. Religious oppression of Protestants by Catholics during the late 17th century was not confined to France. The Mouton fold fled Belgium for Middelburg in Holland. That city was one of two, along with Amsterdam, that was the seat of the Heeren Seventien or the board of directors of the Dutch East India Company (VOC).

By and by they joined the great Huguenot exodus of the 1680s that was funnelled through Holland with the promise of a brighter future, and what could have sounded better than a Cape of Good Hope in sunny Africa? The Mouton family was granted land in Het Land Van Waveren, the Tulbagh Valley, on the eastern slopes of the Elandskloofberge.

Unlike today where men in Cape Town have, apparently, the pick of the women (who, incidentally, are reputed to be the finest in the land), back then men far outnumbered women and so the fairer sex were in a buyer's market. Maria chose as her husband Frans Jooste who farmed on the western slopes of the Elandskloofberge, an area that today is known as the Joostenbergvlakte and is part of the greater Swartland agricultural breadbasket.

Jooste was some twenty years older than Maria. Who knows, having lost her mother so early she was possibly looking for a father figure. Also, it is not implausible that she figured an older man equated with the material security her family had lacked up to that time.

Dry-land farming augured a hard life, but the Cape's was a slave economy so most of the heavy lifting was done by free human machinery. Even so, farming on the sandy and relatively infertile vlakte was a life better suited to its endemic geometric tortoises than it was to the wheat farmers of the area. The Joostenbergvlakte was no luxuriant Constantia Valley where a Meneer Cloete could sit on his stoep looking out to False Bay, a young slave lad dressed in waistcoat and frilly ruff holding the pipe while he smoked and sipped claret, serenaded by a slave ensemble.

During the trial for the crime that was to follow, the only evidence which shines any light on her state of mind was that in around a decade of marriage her husband was so miserly he had not bought her any new clothes. We can imagine Maria living a threadbare life, isolated on a farm that was on the edge of, if not beyond, the pale. However, we know little about her mental state other than that her husband was apparently as parsimonious towards his wife as he was harsh in his treatment of his slaves.

His nickname was Schurfde (Rough) Frans, earned in a time when roughness was the order of the day. It is highly likely that he lifted a hand to his wife from time to time, bearing in mind that that kind of behaviour was widespread and considered an acceptable form of domestic regulation.

Given her aberrant behaviour – no one else during this period is known to have committed a crime considered equally as heinous against the mores of the colonial society – we must assume that either she was unstable in some psychological way beforehand, or that she was driven that way by her husband and the unfortunate condition in which she found herself. What comes to mind is JM Coetzee's disturbing psycho-horror story *In the Heart of the Country* where the central character, very much in the same circumstances as Maria Mouton, grows increasingly paranoid and schizophrenic. Who knows?

What we do know is that, in the years leading up to the final denouement, Maria far preferred the company of the farm slaves than that of her spouse. It was fairly common for the men of the colony to requisition female slaves for their sexual pleasure, but a woman dare not on pain of death – or worse, as we shall find out.

I can certainly see the image of a young woman trapped on a lonely farm in dangerous times, often alone for long periods. In my mind's eye I see her sitting on a shaded stoep, perhaps doing embroidery or, more likely, skinning potatoes. In the field in front of her the slaves are working, their muscles toned by years of hard physical labour, bodies bronzed by a glaze of sweat and covered in only flimsy apparel …

Would that not have been enough to stir something in the spirit of that woman, trapped on a farm in Africa and bound by the puritanical norms of Europe? If the name of that slave happened to be Hercules, Adonis or Titus (as it often was) you can just imagine the resolve of a frustrated and possibly mistreated wife melting in the Cape's relentless summer heat. Such were the circumstances of Maria because we know that two of the slaves owned by Jooste were Titus van Bengal and Fortuijn van Angola. It was Titus that Maria took as her lover.

There were at the time strict rules in place, social codes as well as laws, to regulate the acceptable behaviour and duties of both slaves and their owners. However, being mere possessions, a slave had very little formal recourse for any breaches of those rules against them.

The relationship between slave owners and slaves depended, for the most part, on the character of the owner. Some slaves were worked and beaten to near death and occasionally to death. Others were freed. Anna van Bengal was a freed slave who married the Sergeant of the Castle, Olaf Bergh.

The other side of this coin of human flesh peddling can be found in the court records of the trial for brutality of one burgher Kuuhn. His uncle Johannes Kuuhn testified that the accused had asked him if he could hit one of his uncle's slaves with a spade. "Go ahead," the older man had replied, "I can easily go out and buy a new one" – not a spade, but a slave. Kuuhn had killed the man and received a comparatively light sentence.

In another case one Johann Gebhart found himself in trouble with the law for mistreatment of a chattel. It was during the tenure of the, for the time and relatively speaking, enlightened Governor Ryk Tulbagh. The farmer had beaten the unfortunate slave to death. It was the first time at the Cape that a white slave owner was sentenced to death for the killing of a slave.

Among the unwritten laws of the system was that slaves were expected to be polite and respectful not only to their owners but all colonial gentry. They were also expected to work hard. Why else would you buy a slave, or a draught ox, or a spade?

However, since a slave was a capital investment, it was expected that a slave owner should not punish a slave excessively but only in proportion to his or her offense. For example, if a slave was in any way disobedient the owner should beat or have the slave beaten. It was customary to have one slave whip another while their workmates held them down or looked on.

Among the written laws of the VOC slave code were that all slaves had to be indoors by 10 pm, they could not sing or whistle at night, slaves who stopped in the street to chat should be beaten with canes, a slave who insulted any "freeman" should be flogged and chained, slaves could not ride horses or wagons on public roads – although this rule was policed about as strictly as double parking in Long Street today – but all of that was slave law lite.

A slave who tried to escape – and many did – but was caught, was usually first whipped and then mutilated, which could be branding or having one hand cut off. For even more serious offences, such as striking a slave-holder or attacking their property by burning crops or buildings (which were common forms of resistance), they would be executed. Trials and subsequent punishments were very public affairs, in part as a form of entertainment but also as a very visible form of social regulation.

No form of execution is pleasant, but some are more ghastly than others. Even though the Dutch were not the cruelest of slave-owning societies, still some visitors to the Cape recorded dismay at what they witnessed there. An internet search of the top ten tortures of all time puts the brass bull right up at number one. Under a hollow brass figure a fire was lit and the poor sod inside would be boiled alive. In order to save the witnesses inordinate trauma the victim's tongue was usually cut out beforehand.

Following the brass bull you will find such innovative machinations as the head crusher, the breast ripper, knee splitter and tongue tearer. Another hugely inventive device usually reserved to correct errant behaviour of women was the Judas Cradle. This was a pyramid made from wood and sometimes metal. The victim would have hands bound and legs pulled apart and then they would be lowered vertically onto the sharp point. No matter where the object pierced first, soon enough it would all be as one down there.

My own personal list topper, however, would definitely be the saw. With this one the victim would be suspended upside down from a scaffold, hands bound and legs pulled apart. They would then have their body sawed in two. Imagine, but don't dwell on it for too long.

None of these specific torture devices was used at the Cape in the 18th century. For women, the preferred form of execution was burning. Sometimes they would be partly burned and then strangled (one does wonder about that). For men there were various options on the table including drawing and quartering, the wheel and impalement with often more than one of these together.

They don't sound so bad until you actually visualise what went down. Drawing and quartering started with the four limbs of the sentenced person being partly sawn through. Then the arms and legs would be tied to horses to be pulled apart. Usually the limbless body would be left to bleed very publically to death, if they were not already past breathing by then.

The wheel was a wagon wheel, but an iron grate might be substituted. The poor sod would be bound to the device then beaten with a heavy metal rod until all the major limb bones were smashed. If still alive after all that, the broken dummy might be strangled, burned or beheaded with sometimes two or all three punishments in succession.

Impalement was undoubtedly the greatest crowd pleaser of the day. The victim would be bound hands and feet, the legs prised apart and then lowered onto a sharpened stake. Here the technique, or lack thereof, of the executioner would be critical. Either by design or chance, the way the stake entered the body would determine the duration of suffering. If the point pierced a vital organ death might come in minutes. However, if the upward path of the stake followed the downward path of the spine, and it missed any vital organs, the ordeal could last days.

I tell you all of this not merely for the intellectual edification therein but rather for the bearing it has on our three central characters, Maria, Titus and Fortuijn.

The event that accelerated the action of this story was the unexpected arrival of another *dramatis personae* in this colonial passion play. He was Pieter, a slave originally from Madagascar but more recently absconded from his owner Dirk Bronske on a neighbouring farm. Just imagine how bad things must have been there for him to seek refuge with Schurfde Frans!

Pieter was described in court as being "insolent". He was no shrinking geranium for sure. On one occasion when Jooste whipped him for insubordination, Pieter threatened him with revenge. Maria seized the opportunity, promising to give Pieter his freedom within three years if he would kill her husband. He turned her down.

The court records further reveal that by that time Maria had been "living in concubinage" with the slave Titus for some years. She also allowed the slaves to socialise inside the main farmhouse, even while her husband was living there.

It was an unbearably hot summer afternoon, one of those days when the ameliorating sea breeze abates and the Swartland bakes in the westward sun. The kind that precipitated the arguments, skirmish and deaths of Thibault and Mercutio in Verona on that fateful day in the lives of Romeo and Juliet; the kind that drives reasonable men and women to unreasonable deeds. It was the third day of January in 1714.

Titus was cleaning the threshing floor. Fortuijn was labouring nearby. Suddenly the kitchen door burst open. Maria flew out crying for help as Frans came after her wielding a cane. Acting impulsively,

Titus ran inside the farmhouse and grabbed Frans's musket. It was loaded. He ran outside and fired at the farmer but the lead shot only wounded the intended target. Fortuijn then took up the cudgels, beating Frans to death with a wooden tool handle.

The musket shot echoed through the still, hot Swartland air. A few hours later another neighbour, Isaac Visagie, rode over to check on things. A cursory search for Jooste came up empty (Maria and her two accomplices had dragged the dead man out of sight and covered his blood with sand.) However, since Maria appeared to him to be unconcerned, Visagie eventually left, but his suspicion's had been aroused.

Then another neighbouring farmer popped over to chew the wheat chaff with Frans but found instead his wife drinking wine with three slave men and two slave women, having what appeared to him a fun time all round. Misgivings were uttered to the landdrost in Stellenbosch and a full inquiry was instigated. Frans's body was found not far from the werf, stuffed down a porcupine hole. Maria, Titus and Fortuijn were detained and interred at the Castle of Good Hope.

On 27 April the slave Pieter was apprehended over the mountains in the Land Van Waveren. Because of his past record it was assumed that it was he who had committed the murder, but proof was needed. The wily Dutch captives placed Pieter in one dark cell and Titus in an adjoining one, outside of which they posted a listener. In due course, in the parlance of crime novels, they squealed.

However, the final and most damning part of the evidence emerged only during the trial in August from a most unexpected witness. When called to testify-five-year-old Jacobus, the eldest of two sons born to Maria and Frans, revealed that he had witnessed the entire scene from inside the kitchen. Today that would have been more than enough to prompt guilty convictions all round.

However, things were not so straightforward in those days: confessions needed to be extracted from the guilty. This was done in the "pijnkamer", or torture room of the Castle. Today you can still visit both the pijnkamer as well as the black hole that was used to detain the most serious of criminals. It is a cellar with a long tunnel entrance. Without benefit of a light, the place is dark as hell and damp as purgatory.

Titus and Maria were quick to confess (given the kinds of tortures available, you understand), but Fortuijn held out for some time. Finally, the three co-conspirators were sentenced to execution for murder and Pieter for desertion.

The murder of masters by slaves was certainly not common, but it did occur from time to time, usually following some form of gross mistreatment, but what was most feared in the colony was a slave uprising. There had been two short and ill-fated ones but the fear always lingered that insurrection might become as inflammatory as the fynbos in summer.

Equally as reprehensible to the colonial society was the open affair between Maria and Titus. Appropriate methods of execution were handed down. Cases of white men having sexual relations with slaves, and even fathering offspring, was commonplace and generally overlooked. There are precious few records of white women bearing the children of slaves.

In Nigel Penn's book which prompted my search for the fuller story of Maria Mouton, he writes: "*Her lustful and murderous conduct, her intercourse with a dark-skinned bondsman, was betrayal of both her gender and her social group. Colonial society as a whole was threatened by her actions.*" This makes the double standards of most boardrooms of today seem rather trifling by comparison.

On the first of September 1714 Maria was tied to a stake inside the Castle walls, probably directly in front of De Kat Balcony, in line of sight of the Castle entrance. The Tuynhuys, the main civic building facing Greenmarket Square, was built only some years later, when the square became the new focus of justice and punishment.

First she was half strangled, then "blackened" (*blaker*) or scorched and finally, while in excruciating pain, strangled to death. It was a didactic show designed to warn the white women of the Cape not to succumb to the allures of all the bronzed, sweat-glazed men that surrounded them at every turn. Maria Mouton was the only white woman executed at the Cape in the eighteenth century.

For his sins Fortuijn was broken on the wheel, and we have seen what that would have entailed, but the demise of Titus was the main attraction. He was sentenced to be impaled. Hands and feet bound, he was positioned with the dreaded sharpened stake up his rectum and left for gravity to do its inexorable work.

His was not one of the quick deaths often described. Around the forth hour of his suffering a sympathetic onlooker proffered him a bottle of arak (what today we would call witblits), with a plea for him not to drink too much too quickly lest he get drunk. He gamely replied that it would not matter since he sat fast enough. There was no fear of his falling off, he assured the crowd.

It would be another forty-four hours before he took his last breath, oxygen ceased to flow to his brain and his heart stopped beating. All that time, or at least for an appreciable period thereof, he kept up his witty banter. At one time he confessed to the onlookers that he would never again trust a woman.

That done, his head and one hand were cut off, as were those of Fortuijn, and they, together with the blackened body of Maria, were placed on poles and exhibited outside the Castle for all to see.

You can read all this and much more about the early Cape in the Journals of HCV Leibrandt, Keeper of the Cape Archives around the beginning of the 20th century. They were published in 1906 by the Cape Times Limited (Cape Town and London) and printed by the Government Printer in Keerom Street. You'll find them inside the national archives on Roeland Street.

Easier to access, however, is the wonderful website The First Fifty Years Project in which many of the most interesting stories scanned from the old Cape archives are shared. There is also a Facebook page of the same name, where the regular posts by Mansell Upham make for highly entertaining and revealing reading. They beat the cat selfies every time.

Coenraad De Buys – Father of a Small Nation

The amazing life and times of the giant, frontiersman, renegade and Bastard King of South Africa

WHO KNEW SOUTH AFRICA HAD its own mythic character, a veritable titan who bestrode the veld more than two hundred years ago? One explorer who met him described him as a South African Hercules. He was by all accounts a giant of a man, a natural leader of men and seducer of women. He was the confidant of kings and consort of queens. The father of a people still today known as the Buysvolk, or Buys Nation. And yet today he is to be found only as an afterthought in some mildewed history books.

I first became aware of the man in the pages of that doorstopper *Frontiers* by Noel Mostert, a one thousand three hundred-odd page tome on the history of the Xhosa-speaking peoples. It was rumoured to have been Madiba's favourite book.

He appears only briefly on that stage as one of the main rabble rousers among the Trekboers of the Eastern Cape, and is thereafter reduced to a few footnotes. However, one of Mostert's footnotes – in *Travels in South Africa between 1803 and 1806* written by adventurer-naturalist Henry Lichtenstein – gave me an early break. Years before I had tracked down a copy of this two-volume set of travel memoirs, published in 1938 by the Van Riebeeck Society, on a rare books auction website.

When I eagerly opened them there he was, standing seven feet tall in his unstockinged velskoens, meeting with Lichtenstein and General Janssens of the short-lived but commendable stab at an egalitarian society in the Cape that we remember as the Batavian Republic. This was the brief interlude between the two British occupations of the Cape when, under Governor De Mist, the Cape offered a semblance of democracy to all, other than slaves.

Janssens was on a tour of the Cape's troubled eastern borderlands with two goals. The first and major one was to try to understand, untangle and resolve the conflicts between black, brown and white in the Zuurveld, that troubled and contested chunk of grazing land between the Sundays and the Great Fish rivers.

The second was to try to meet with the giant (De Buys) and offer him a pardon from the price that had been put on his head by The Company for his role as the leader of "a rebellious cabal" of burghers of Bruitjieshoogte (the district around Graaff-Reinet) who were set on fomenting strife between the various groups, mostly with the intention of furthering their own land-grabbing and cattle-rustling ways.

De Buys, together with his co-conspirators, the Prinsloos and Bezuidenhouts, had got a very bad press back in Cape Town. When Janssens, Lichtenstein and entourage caught up with him somewhere between the Fish and Kei rivers in December of 1803, the colossal Trekboer had the worst kind of reputation, but Lichtenstein saw something different in the man.

"He was invited to meet us and came on the thirty-first of December. The representations which rumour, too much addicted to exaggeration, had given us beforehand of this extraordinary man, were corrected from the moment of his entrance."

The adventurer noted their guest's uncommon height, his obvious strength and admirable physique and carriage as well as a certain dignity of movement "such one might conceive to have been the heroes of ancient times; he seemed to be the living figure of Hercules."

As the meeting progressed and Janssens discussed the deteriorating situation on the Eastern Frontier between white settlers, indigenous Khoi, black pastoralists and the armies of Cape Town, Lichtenstein observed in the rough frontiersman a modesty and restraint that was quite at odds with his odious reputation.

When questioned he delivered answers with slow deliberation behind which was a "sort of significant smile" that implied, the writer says, a self-knowledge of his own considerable powers and influence among his fellow frontiersmen as well as with the indigenous people among whom he moved. In this, Lichtenstein observed, could be read "that his forbearance was not the result of fear, but that he scorned to satisfy curiosity of any one at the expense of truth or of his own personal reputation".

He willingly gave information when questioned by the General, but was most reluctant to speak of his time and relationship with Xhosa Chief Ngqika (also known as Gaika) and the chief's mother. And that, says the peregrinacious scribe, made him so much more believable and gaining of sympathy than would have been the case had he simply attempted to excite his audience with tales of his own escapades. Lichtenstein was the only biographer of De Buys who actually met him.

Mostert, by contrast, describes the subject as being wild, cunning, sly, brutal and ambiguous, but then his main sources for his humungous work were the records of various missionaries working along the Cape's outermost reaches. They mostly all detested everything the frontiersman stood for, except for one very queer fish of an evangelist.

Johannes van der Kemp was sent to the Cape by the London Mission Society and arrived among the black people east of the Kei River sans shoes or even sun hat. In that sense he might be regarded as the original "rooinek". It set him well apart from all the other white people they had yet seen and this gave him a bit of a foot in their door. They, already bemused by the white people piling up on their doorsteps and not trusting them one bit, did not know what to make of this pared-down white man.

Van der Kemp was, to use an ironic figure of speech, on a mission. Misdeeds in his past back in Holland – he was reprimanded there by none less than the Prince of Orange for leading an unsavoury life – had set him on a personal and fanatical pilgrimage which alienated him from just about everyone else, white and black, military and missionary.

He set up God's shop near Chief Ngqika's kraal, or "great place", eschewing virtually all earthly comforts, hammering relentlessly on the rock-hard ground of salvation. He turned his cheek to all manner of abuse, thievery, slander, assault and threat. One thing he never did was waiver. It was all part of God's plan for him and but small trials and tribulations to be borne in order to atone for his sins.

Van der Kemp and the black chief's white advisor, who at that stage was also living at Ngqika's great place in the Tymie Valley, in the foothills of the Amatola Mountains below Hogsback, became close friends. They were both two curious outsiders, but they were also alike in another way.

De Buys is known to have consorted only with women of colour. Van der Kemp married a freed slave woman, Sarah Janse, forty-five years his junior. For this, as well as for compiling dossiers of ill-treatment against the white settlers, he was recalled to the Cape by his missionary masters. He was the first white person to make serious studies of both the Khoi and Xhosa languages.

Perhaps the hardest thing to understand is how De Buys, who championed the cause of the Trekboers and was willing to take up arms with the rebels against the Cape for their right to push back the frontier and claim land (and often the cattle they took, stole, or won) as theirs, could also live among the Xhosa people and become not only their advisor but often their champion in various battles.

His reputation grew and most likely was exaggerated, but who was this man of myth and misunderstanding all but lost in the musty pages of state archives? To understand just how this larger-than-life character came to be there in the first place requires we go back to the beginning.

Coenraad De Buys was born in 1761 on the farm Wagenboomrivier near Montagu, "beyond Cogmanskloof", one of around eight homesteads that by then had been built in the Little Karoo. His father Jan was the scion of a well-to-do family of wine growers who had been Huguenot settlers from Calais. Jan married a Dutch woman, Christina Minnie, and moved east with the Trekboer pioneers. By the time De Buys was born the family had fallen on hard times. He was put to work from a very early age, herding his father's stock and doing menial tasks.

At the age of seven he spent a night watching his father curled up in agony, slowly dying. In the morning, the old man still and cold, De Buys packed whatever few possessions he had and walked to the farm of his half-sister Getruy and her husband Dawid Senekal. Getruy told him she had seen another man die that same way, Gert Minnie, her own father who had been married to Christina at the time. Just six months later Christina married Dawid Senekal's younger brother Jacob.

De Buys lived with Getruy and Dawid as a *knecht*, or unpaid labourer. The next we hear of him is in the court records of the VOC (the Dutch East India Company, fastidious record keepers) where he sued his brother-in-law over a business venture carting butter to Cape Town. It seems De Buys, ever quick to anger and take offence, did not understand or appreciate the matter of a credit account.

He lost the case and so upped and offed and we next find him tending a loan farm near the Bushman's River on the Eastern Frontier. There he became involved with a Baster-Khoi woman of slave descent, Maria van der Horst, who in time bore him seven children. One source implies that his early life among the pioneer farmers of the Little Karoo and Langkloof was harsh and brutal and was why De Buys found his way to other communities that offered him more comfort.

In most ways De Buys was a typical frontiersman – fiercely

independent to the point of defiance. Also typical of the Trekboers of the time, he was a restless soul and soon we find him again stirring the pot. Records show he did not pay the taxes or rental due to The Company. Then he, along with a bunch of other rebels of the contested Zuurveld region, easily fell in with the time-honoured African custom of raiding cattle from the Xhosa clans they bumped up against – in the case of De Buys, their women as well. He is thought to have fathered more than three hundred children with women of every colour except white.

The Dutch East India Company continually tried to keep the peace on the frontier, but it was extremely hard to enforce the law let alone untangle the cause and nature of the skirmishes so far from the seat of authority in Cape Town. It was always a case of tit-for-tat. Because of his great size and bearing, De Buys was a natural leader to whom dispossessed people flocked – rebels, runaways and rogues all, to quote historian Nigel Penn.

Together, and as often separately, they repeatedly roused the local settler populace to take up arms against the Cape (one of these was the infamous uprising that terminated with the multiple hangings at Slagtersnek). They were also frequently identified as the perpetrators of brutal beatings of slaves as well as Khoi and black labourers on their farms.

Chief Langa had a long-running dispute with De Buys, complaining that he regularly crossed the Fish River – at the time the official colonial boundary – to steal cattle. When the white man stole the Xhosa chief's wife, or one of them, and then sought refuge with his rival, Chief Ngqika, it set the two traditional chiefs against one another. This enmity would have severe consequences for all and became the flash point for numerous clashes.

As pressure mounted to bring him to law, Khula ("the big one", as the Xhosa dubbed De Buys) moved his entire entourage of wives, children, servants, as well as numerous other followers and their families, to Ngqika's "great place". Here the big man took to the chief's apparently heroically corpulent mother, Yese, becoming her consort as well as the chief's most senior advisor.

The men in ruffs and silver buckled shoes back at the Castle in

Cape Town were not impressed. What Maria van der Horst thought of this arrangement, and of the many others that followed, is not recorded. However, Yese frequently sought to bring De Buys back to her ample bosom whenever he strayed and betimes constructed her own intrigues in order to variously punish or reward him.

Then, in rather rapid succession, things in Cape Town changed. The VOC was bankrupted by wars between Holland and England. The English, fearing French control of the Cape, took possession in 1795. A huge naval and ground force invaded at Muizenberg and met with little resistance from Sergeant Muys and his small force, which moved out of range of the British guns to Retreat (now a suburb adjacent to Muizenberg). They surrendered soon afterwards, but the Brits stayed for only a few years and when they departed they left a political vacuum that was filled by the short-lived Batavian Republic of Governor De Mist and General Janssens.

It was at this point that Janssens met with and offered De Buys a pardon, which he accepted. De Buys, with his family and closest allies, moved back west to the frontier settler community around Bruintjieshoogte, the centre of which was the town of Graaff-Reinet.

The next time we meet up with him is in the court records of George (the town named in honour of King George II) after the British had returned and retaken the Cape in 1806 at the Battle of Blaauwberg. The records show that De Buys got embroiled in a case against the settler farmers, Thomas and Martha Ferreira. Martha in particular was accused of having grossly mistreated slaves and servants, allegedly killing one of them by repeated beatings.

De Buys, no light hand with whip or rod, was brought in as a state witness against the Ferreiras. The couple was found not guilty on almost all counts (Martha claimed the female slave Manissa had succumbed to "Mozambican sickness"). But this set De Buys against the sentiments of the other settlers and he found himself alienated from them. And so, once more, he packed his wagons and turned them eastwards to renew his life among the indigenous tribes.

The next detour in his story is vague at best. At some point, it is not clear exactly when, he went on a reconnaissance northwards into the land of the Tembus and, some references claim, as far as the land of the Zulus. When he returned it was with a black wife who is only ever referred to as Elizabeth.

Various sources say she was "taken" from a minor Tembu chief, while others claim she was the sister of the Zulu general and later founder of the Ndebele nation in Zimbabwe, Mzilikazi. If that was the case, he would not have been able to abduct her and return with his skin still on his body without Mzilikazi's approval.

Elizabeth seems to have replaced Maria van der Horst as De Buys's favourite wife. We hear less and less of Maria and more and more of the Xhosa or Zulu wife and her children. It is likely that, whatever the fate of Maria, the children she had with De Buys had grown up and drifted off to find their own fortunes, while the younger ones he had with Elizabeth stuck with them to the end of this tale. They had many children together.

During the second British occupation of the Cape, De Buys was among many of the Dutch-speaking population who sought to distance themselves from these unwelcome new masters. De Buys, the tallest poppy in the veld, attracted undue attention and once again found himself with a price on his head, accused of being the prime instigator of conflict between Xhosa and British (this much is almost certainly true).

De Buys's entourage, now including British military deserters, decided to look for new lands way beyond the reach of the colony. They trekked northwestwards over the Karoo interior, across Bushmanland, to reach the Orange River in 1812 or 1813. Here "the big one" fell in with other brigands and fugitives from the colony, including fellow Boers, Basters, Griquas, Koranna, Oorlam Afrikanders, Khoi, Tswana and even Xhosa refugees.

By that time a rival group of Boer renegades had already set up what Lichtenstein described as a "state in miniature". They vied for turf along the green oasis of the Orange River where there was a Khoi-Griqua army of raiders led by a German mercenary, Jan Bloem. There were also various other groups of desperados. It was as wild a west as ever there was.

De Buys's reputation grew as he marauded through areas where the London Missionary Society was active, under resolute men such as Moffat, Philip and Campbell. They in turn sent a continual narrative of events back to their mission society bosses and acted as the Colony's eyes and ears in the borderlands. With few exceptions, these men of the cloth saw themselves as the sharp end of righteous European expansion into Africa. Not everyone agreed.

With that tantalising price on his head again, De Buys found himself continually hounded by anyone and everyone hell-bent on taking him dead or alive. I am reminded here of the part in the film *Butch Cassidy and the Sundance Kid*, where they are pursued relentlessly across the Americas by a "Pinkerton man" in a bowler hat.

He skipped ahead of them, sometimes by the narrowest of escapes, and eventually left the Orange River area. He steered his troupe along the Molopo River into the lands of Setswana-speaking people. Makaba was one of numerous Tswana chiefs with whom De Buys sought refuge as he fled one step ahead of the bounty hunters. There were many rumours of his death from around this time, all proved untrue.

Between 1815 and 1820, warlords including Mzilikazi and the Amazonian Mantisi were ravaging the region. Today we know this period as the Difaqane when the rise of warlords in east and central southern Africa laid waste to the interior and decimated the population, many small tribes and clans being wiped out or incorporated into the larger ones. Some resorted to living like early *Homo sapiens* in forest refuges while others resorted to living in caves and practising cannibalism.

As he moved ever further into the unknown, De Buys found his troubles increasing. He was so far from home and frequently found himself short on crucial resources such as gunpowder and shot. When he was in supply he was an invaluable ally against the ravaging hordes, but when he was out he found himself at great risk.

By and by his horses died, his cattle were taken by various chiefs as "gifts", tributes or levies for crossing their lands and all too often his firearms as well. At one point he was held prisoner by Chief Makaba. He released De Buys only when news reached his kraal of other white people approaching, fearing they were coming to the rescue.

He need not have feared for it was the missionary John Campbell on the trail of De Buys on behalf of Graaff-Reinet landrost, Andries Stockenström. De Buys assumed the landrost was on his trail in order to detain him and drag him back to the colony to face the law and so, as soon as he was able, De Buys packed and skedaddled.

In truth Stockenström was keen to welcome the fugitive back into the fold with a pardon. As often as he could, he relayed messages ahead to this effect. Whether or not the marauding frontiersman got the messages, or whether he did and ignored them, we will never know. Maybe he was just so far gone into the wilderness and, like Mr Kurtz lost to demons in the Congo jungle, there was no going back.

In one of the many reports penned by missionary John Campbell he says: "Buys, the Africaner, is reported to sleep little, being always afraid of an attack upon his life. He has three guns, which he keeps beside him, and has taught his wife (Elizabeth) how to load them, that when attacked, he may have only to fire. He is a miserable man, and his family is captive with him. Had we accepted of Makaba an invitation to visit him at Melita, it is very probable the whole party would have been detained."

Freed and determined to retain his independence, De Buys now led his increasingly dispirited party on a course northeastwards. They had few cattle left, all their horses were dead, their ammunition exhausted and the big man had resorted to hunting with a bow and arrows.

Somewhere along the Limpopo River, Elizabeth died of yellow fever. This seems to have been a last straw. Some forty or fifty years later his son Michael de Buys (by that stage the leader of the clan) recalled that in the end his father seemed to have lost his spirit. He certainly had lost almost all his possessions – wagons, cattle, horses, guns – along with his physical strength and most of his teeth.

Around 1820 his bedraggled party, dubbed the Buysvolk, settled in a place now shown on maps as Buysstad. In the shadow of the Soutpansberg range Coenraad De Buys set off on his final trek. He left his party in the care of his oldest remaining son Michael (one of Elizabeth's children). They were to await his return at the kraal of

Chief Kgahdi. Setting off due east he rode upon his last trek ox … and that is the last that was ever seen or heard of him.

And so this man who was a legend in his own lifetime simply walked (or rode) off the pages of history and into the realm of mythology. Eighteen years later the Voortrekker party led by Louis Trichardt reached the area and set up one of the first Boer independencies, although it did not last very long.

Buysstad lies somewhere midway between present day Louis Trichardt and Dendron. You could drive through without noticing it. The Buysvolk formed a distinct community, but time has rendered them indistinguishable from the Venda, Tswana and Pedi people of the region. De Buys's progeny have swelled from a few hundred to several thousand.

Finding Lichtenstein's work quoted in *Frontiers* was the key into the mansion of Coenraad De Buys, but it was a dark house and I would need more light to venture further down the corridors and into interior rooms. Among Mostert's bibliography were two other references, Schoeman and Millin. I remembered Sarah Gertrude Millin as a novelist of an earlier time spoken about by my parents, but it was only a vague memory.

So I turned to Professor Google and found Millin's book, *King of the Bastards*. However, getting it into my hands proved to be a somewhat more convoluted venture. It's been out of print since the 1950s and several enquiries came up empty. I eventually found a copy in a second-hand book dealership in Youngstown, Missouri, USA. After an arduous journey across continents and seas, it finally reached me.

I read it with urgency, but became increasingly disillusioned to find it was a highly romanticised story bedeviled by the bigotry of Millin's age. Meanwhile my hunt for the work of Ms Schoeman continued. The journey started at my local municipal library. They directed me to the provincial reference library which, I learned, was not a lending library, but they sent me onwards to the state library in the Company Gardens. There, among the muted chambers and columns of the rare books collection – having completed the requisite paperwork – I was able to read the entire manuscript under the watchful eyes of our nation's finest librarians, bless them. What a read!

Coenraad de Buys: The First Transvaler by Agatha Elizabeth Schoeman (born Kingdon) was submitted in partial fulfillment for a degree of Master of Arts in the Faculty of Arts at the University of Pretoria in 1938. The copy I had was one of only two known to exist in South Africa, outside of any private collection. The thesis does not thank anyone or explain how she came upon her subject, but the bibliography makes for tantalising reading: historians Fuller and Theal, explorers Baines, Burchell, Barrow and Lichtenstein (of course), missionaries Van der Kemp (naturally) and Campbell (always) among the many historical documentarians.

There were references from Fairburn and Pringle's *South African Journal* and finally the real antiquities and treasures – the Cape Archives and various "blue books", reports of various commissions on the "native tribes" of South Africa and conflicts on the Eastern Frontier. Schoeman had scoured the records of the old Cape Parliament, the records of the VOC and every pertinent book on early Cape history whether written in Dutch, German or English. As a former student of South African media history, this was literary candy.

She opens her account with a character reference that sets the high scholarly tone of her thesis: "The blood of French refugees and of the pioneer Dutch colonists met in Coenraad de Buys, and this blending produced in him a man in whom the characteristics of both races were intensified almost to a fault."

Was there ever such a man as Coenraad De Buys: pioneer, adventurer, vagabond, bandit and Hercules? Schoeman calls him "the first Transvaler" but I have come to think of him as the first authentic South African. By taking sides with and against just about everyone, and taking sexual partners from Khoi, Xhosa and possibly Zulu groups, he and his progeny were truly of "rainbow" or multi-racial character.

Dart and Boshier – Two Peas in a Peculiar Pod

The remarkable collaboration between an anatomist and an antagonist

THROUGHOUT HISTORY THERE HAVE been remarkable collaborations where the resulting whole was exponentially greater than the mere sum of the parts: think of the Wright brothers, Lennon and McCartney, Page and Brin. South Africa has Mandela and Mbeki, Clegg and Mchunu, Zuma and Gupta.

One of the more remarkable if unlikely collaborations on our soil was between a world-famous doctor and a maverick bushwacker. The doctor was Raymond Dart, professor of anatomy at the University of the Witwatersrand and discoverer of the famous prehistoric Taung fossil skull. The other was Adrian Boshier, wanderer, shaman and general malcontent.

This is a story about the meeting between these two unlikely partners but also a meeting of different cultures. It is a story about time – past, present and future – a meeting of time zones. In order to be comfortable in your velskoens, izicathulo or whatever you wear on your feet when you perambulate the plains where our pre-human ancestors walked, you need to appreciate African time.

African time recognises the present as being a central point of reference, with past and future receding outward like ripples. We, the living, are the connection between the dead, the shades, and those not yet born. The characters in this story appear to me to be ripples that glimmer as their shadows pass over my own fluid surface, but I'll get back to that.

Raymond Arthur Dart was born in Brisbane, Australia, in 1893. He studied medicine in Sydney and served as a captain in the Australian medical corps during World War I. A biography states that after that war he "reluctantly" took up a position in the newly established Department of Anatomy at Wits University in Johannesburg.

Just two years into the job, in 1924, he received two crates containing fossil bones from a limeworks in Taung, a dorp that straddles the border of the Northern Cape and North West provinces due north of Kimberley. It proved to be the turning point of his life. Among those bones was a small fossil skull. Dart realised it had to be that of an early hominid, given its archaic outer shape and a brain case that was too large to be that of either a baboon or chimpanzee.

The skull had been kept as an ornament on the mantelpiece above the fireplace in the home of Pat Izod, son of the director of the limeworks. While it is true that Dart first correctly identified and described it, its discovery (cited by some in the know as the most important anthropological fossil find of the twentieth century) parallels that of Watson and Crick and the woman who actually first identified the DNA double helix pattern, Rosalind Franklin, who did not get to share the limelight or the Nobel Prize that followed.

It was a student of Dart's, his very first in fact, Josephine Salmons, who appreciated the mantelpiece decoration as something unusual. She persuaded the people at the limeworks to send it and other fossil bones to Dart. Some time later the solid endocast (the inside volume of the brain case), with the imprint of the cranial vault of the same skull was found being used as a paperweight by the limeworks manager.

Dart   named   the   newly   discovered   ape-man   species

Australopithecus africanus. Due to its diminutive size it has forthwith been known as the Taung child. However, because Dart was working in Africa and not Europe (naturally, higher hominid evolution must be focused there!), and because he was not a member of the accepted scientific community of the day, his find was pretty much ignored by the world beyond. It would take the concerted work of another leading paleoanthropologist working in South Africa at the time, Dr Robert Broom (who we meet again in the chapter on James Kitching), to vindicate Dart's finding and place South Africa at the centre of the search for our ancestors.

While delving into the dark secrets of our earliest known forebears, Dart had something of an epiphany. The description of the so-called Stone Ages did little to explain who those people were and how they might have lived, he argued. He proposed a new human age, an "osteodontokeratic" culture.

Dart postulated that they used not stones as their first tools, and certainly never exclusively, but what they used mostly were bone, teeth and horn. Especially in places like the Kalahari were there were no stones. Hunter gatherers would use all the more unyielding parts of an animal as tools, including hides, sinews, hair and, of course, bone, horn and teeth.

One of Dart's interests was the study of the structure of brains. First human brains but, following the discovery of the Taung skull, also pre-human and reptile. In reptiles he identified the primordial neocortex, the oldest part of the brain – any brain – that can be recognised as being part of the cerebral cortex (what we refer to as grey matter, the thinking parts).

Branching off into the shadowy world of speculative anthropology, guided largely by tooth architecture, and working with other leading paleoanthropologists of the day, he hypothesised that our primate ancestors had been at least partially meat eaters and therefore killer apes. American playwright, screen and science writer Robert Ardrey (who had a background in geology and paleontology) was the first popular and internationally recognised figure to fall in with the South African way of thinking.

On a trip to South Africa in 1955 he met Dart who, by that time, had amassed more than five thousand fossil bones and many ancient artefacts. Something like ninety per cent of them were the lower jaw bones of antelope, which could be used as cutting tools, as well as the humeri of large herbivores, which could be used as clubs.

In his most famous books on the subject, *African Genesis* and *The Territorial Imperative*, Ardrey proposed that mankind had been born in Africa and that we were natural killers. Both propositions were highly contentious at the time, but slowly they gained wider appreciation, if not open acceptance.

It was around this time that a colleague knocked on the office door of Raymond Dart, saying there was a man who wanted to talk to him about the artefacts on display in the adjoining room; someone he'd met, spellbound by his travel stories, insisted he had to pay a visit to the renowned professor. Dart found a taciturn, tall, thin, young man, direct to the point of being abrasive, poring over the various items.

"I know those," said the younger man without the nicety of an introduction. Dart's heart leaped. It was a fossil tibial bone shaped like a tool, like a knife. It was one of the pieces central to Dart's long-held theory about the social and cultural evolution of our species, but so far he had not been able to find any connecting thread between the primitive bone tools and any known human culture.

"I've got one ..." Well, you could have knocked over the greying academic with the humerus of a very small antelope. Here was not only his link, but also a person who could prove his theory, he more than hoped.

Adrian Boshier was born in Wiltshire the year that World War II began. In 1955, when the boy was sixteen, his family left dulled, war-ravaged England for Africa, settling in Johannesburg. During his early teens, as a means of escaping the gloomy English weather and the general depression of the post-war years, Boshier had consumed everything he could find about the early British adventurers in Africa – notably Livingstone, Stanley and Selous.

On reaching his long dreamed of Africa it was only a few months before he took the great leap forward: at a party someone announced they'd be leaving for the bushveld in the morning. The teenager grabbed a rucksack into which he threw a few possessions and jumped in the car.

Years later the driver recalled that no sooner had they left behind the bright lights of the golden city than his young passenger began nagging: "Are we there yet, are we there yet?" Eventually the man, tiring of the onslaught, said "yes". Boshier ordered him to stop and let him out. For the rest of his days on this mortal earth Adrian Boshier lived wholly or partially as an eardstapper, a wanderer, someone who is, in the literature of Olde English, "a pilgrim or one who seeks a meaning beyond the temporary and transitory meaning of earthly values".

For six full years he walked alone. He slept on the ground or in caves when he could find them. He lived by catching wild things, snails and lizards, snakes and bats. He wandered the bushveld of an area then known as the Northern Transvaal. It was the realm of the North Sotho people, who could be divided and divided again into various tribal groups speaking Sotho and Tswana but also Pedi and Venda.

Someone who knew the tall, thin man well described him as looking like a stork. However, having seen photos and even old movies of him, I see him as a secretary bird, striding the veld with those long legs, a large beak-like nose, his dishevelled hair resembling the distinguishing feathers on the head of *Sagittarius serpentarius*, the long-legged snake eagle.

Prior to setting off on his great walkabout, an incident occurred that was to set him up for the destiny and reputation that awaited. He was ambling around a municipal golf course one day when he encountered a large rinkhals or ring-necked spitting cobra that was quite common on the Highveld in those days. He felt compelled to act, as if this was a test sent for him to prove himself.

Wanting to bear down on the snake, but knowing it possessed a deadly arsenal, he circled the serpent. The snake reared up, spread its hood while in and out its forked tongue flicked. It was a large specimen, well over a metre long and thick as the boy's arm. The snake had been lying in the rough, where Adrian was able to find a stick suitably shaped so he could break it and create a fork. The deadly dance continued, Boshier wary of a possible venom stream directed at his eyes.

Eventually he managed to pin down the cobra's head, grab its thrashing body and restrain it using all his might. Snakes are strange though: after an initial demonic struggle, once they realise they are well and truly restrained, they seem to give up the fight and become quite tame. Rinkhalses are also known to put on a very believable dead act, but not this time.

He later recalled: "I have never again had to exert such will and nerve. Bending down and grasping that snake behind the head was the most difficult thing I have ever had to do." This incident is recorded in the biography about Boshier, *The Lightning Bird* written by Lyall Watson, after his untimely death.

Boshier made acquaintance with white farmers in the Waterberg district and accepted their hospitality as a means of moving onward. In the early years he believed he was travelling alone, but later he found that the veld is full or eyes and ears. The jungle drums hummed and news spread before him. It was also observed that he regularly caught snakes, including the most dangerous ones.

To an African a snake is not just a snake. It is believed that snakes are powerful embodiments of ancestral spirits and anyone who catches them harnesses their power.

Whenever Boshier approached kraals or villages that had a snake problem, emissaries would reach him first and ask him to come and exorcise their place. The time that he wrestled with and subdued a massive black mamba that was troubling a village sealed his reputation as a man with deep and strong links to the ancestral spirits, the *badimo*.

Another time, Boshier caught a very large python, which took him some hours to subdue. He then walked into the nearest village with it draped over his lanky frame. The people fled. This incident earned him his African nick-name, or totem really, Rradinokga – the father of snakes.

The fact that Adrian Boshier suffered epilepsy was, to the African people, further proof of his immense spiritual powers. There is a tradition among African shamans (call them witchdoctor, ngaka, sangoma or whatever you will) be they Khoi, Zulu or Sotho. One method of divining for them is to perform a trance dance where, in short, they hallucinate in order to speak with the spirits. Upon going into the trance state they appear to suffer great pain, doubling over, falling to the ground, sometimes right into the trance dance fire, and writhe as if in agony.

It looks a lot like someone suffering from an epileptic fit. Epileptics are thought to have especial powers, conferred on them by the ancestors, that allow them to go into "trance" fits without having undergone the strict and protracted initiation and training required to become a shaman. Rradinokga ... clearly here was a man upon whom the shades had conferred special favour.

Still, at first the black people of the bushveld could not work him out, a white man walking alone in the veld. White people just didn't do that. The drums spoke of this crazy mlungu who walked, village to village, with nothing but what was in his bag or pockets, a blanket, pocket knife and a bag of salt. He ate what the black people did and drank their fermented sorghum beer or marula beer in season, as well as their water scooped from containers with a calabash. They knew no other white person who would ever do *that*.

An important development for Boshier came when he found he could actually make a living, meagre as it was, walking the veld. Laboratories were willing to pay him to supply snake and scorpion venom, so now he had a paying profession and was no longer just a wandering bum. However, it was the day in 1962 when he first met Professor Dart that catapulted him onto a higher trajectory.

"... oh yes," the younger man continued, "I use it all the time."

How, when, where? the older man wanted to know. Boshier began to regale him with his knowledge of this old knife culture. He explained that if you should travel through the bushveld (the savanna region north of Pretoria and south of the Limpopo), you would notice in the tribal areas that just about every field has a tree. Not just any tree, but a marula tree (*Sclerocarya birrea*).

The sweet, golden apricot-sized fruits of the marula ripen in February and March. At this time work pretty much comes to a halt. Everyone collects the fruits, each tree belonging to a particular kraal or person. You could say northern Sotho was a marula culture. Women sit in the shade of a tree gossiping, using a bone knife to scoop out the hard pip and then place the juicy pith into a container. The fruit ferments in just a day or two, producing a delicious fruity champagne, *méthode Afrique classique* redolent with the fragrance of apricots and African dust.

The marula fruit is deemed to be a gift from the gods. They, in turn, have to be respected and treated in the way of the ancestors. No metal may be used in processing them. Only a bone knife, as it has been since time before time, specifically a sharpened tibial bone of a cow or antelope.

Marula time is fiesta time in the bushveld with a party under every tree. You cannot move about the region without some serious chin-wagging and heavy elbow lifting. Incidentally, it is only female trees that bear fruit, while male trees produce flowers and supply the pollen for procreation.

Dart realised that in Boshier he had been delivered someone with a special gift he needed, even though Dart himself was something of a sorcerer. He read bones, old bones, and in them peered deep into the past, but here was someone who could provide that living link with the past he had perceived.

He offered the brash young man a job as an assistant working for the Museum of Man and Science (no connection to the muti shop of the same name now found in Diagonal Street). Boshier was to be his eyes and ears in the veld. The professor briefed his new recruit what he was to look out for, what questions to ask on his ramblings, and what to read to give him a firm background footing in his (Dart's) field of expertise. Systematically, fibre by fibre, they began to put the flesh back onto those old bones.

The job gave Boshier a new sense of purpose. This, at last, seemed to be his calling and he would disappear into the bush without notice, only to reappear at some unspecified time later without so much as a dispatch. In time he married and fathered two sons, but the marriage could not survive his insatiable, incurable searching. During this time he became apprenticed to a very powerful sangoma in the Makgabeng hills, outliers of the Waterberg range.

He was shown singing stones, such as can be found throughout sub-Saharan Africa. They are never random but produce pure harmonic notes when the smoothly polished indentations are struck with special stone hammers. With the help of another powerful ngaka he was the first person to unpeel the layers of meanings underpinning rock art in the region.

He uncovered the significance of red ochre – the blood of the earth – in the ancient rituals of Africa, as well as in ancient mines of the sub-continent. His most significant singular discovery though was probably finding the sacred ancestral drums of the Matala people of Makgabeng.

These were the dikomama or rain-making drums that had been hidden by the keeper of the drums back in the 1880s when urged by the arrival of European missionaries to abandon their ancient ways of worship. On his return from secreting the drums in a deep cave with only a sliver of an entrance, the old drummer had been kicked on the head by one of his bulls and died before he could share their location with anyone else.

Prior to Boshier's arrival the area had been gripped in the vice of terrible drought. The people were despondent and starving. With the return of the drums a great ceremony was held. That night rain clouds massed and it rained copiously. This part concerning the tribe of Makgabeng is worth telling at greater length for it is fascinating and revelationary but I think I will keep it for another day and another book.

Adrian Boshier could have become a truly great shaman but, as his sangoma teacher found, he just could not keep still. And you need to be still to properly hear the spirits. Some people believe it was his epilepsy that drove him so relentlessly, driven by his own demons. He died while snorkelling on a trip to Sodwana Bay in 1978. Not by drowning mind you, but a heart attack. The person who was first to the struggling man in the water noted he had a smile, and his last words were, "well that wasn't so bad".

I had heard about this crazy character called Adrian Boshier from my mother, a nurse and keen amateur anthropologist. Born in a railway shack, she was an unapologetic and enthusiastic social climber. I learned who was who on the ridge of gold from her name-dropping anecdotes: Fitzpatrick and Niven, Broom and Dart, Tobias and Boshier. They became the colourful backdrop characters in the theatre of my adolescence.

When she died I inherited many of her books, notably those by Eugène Marais, Robert Ardrey and Lyall Watson. I discovered Watson had been a teacher at my primary school. He never taught me but I suspect that had he, I might now be a white-coated scientist sorting through ancient artefacts. I also found that while growing up in Johannesburg and later living in Cape Town, the Boshiers had lived not just once but four times "just around the corner" from my own family.

Raymond Dart outlived his protégé. He died in Johannesburg in 1988 in a retirement home owned and run by my mother. She was extremely proud of her celebrity resident, as am I of an artwork of a rampaging elephant that hangs, pride of place, on our dining room wall. I think it is a side story worth including.

On a visit to Nieu Bethesda some years ago I noticed two minutely detailed pencil drawings of bushveld scenes, each about A4 in size, hanging in the local art gallery. I couldn't resist them. It was only when I got back home and took out a magnifying glass to the works that I was able to make out the name of the artist, rendered in fine cursive pencil script: Bowen Boshier. Not a common surname, could there be a connection?

Years of searching bore no fruit. Until one day on a morning stroll I bumped into him and his wife. They lived around the corner from me in Cape Town. It turned out that from his father, Adrian Boshier, he had inherited a wandering spirit and deeply perceptive eye. From his mother (a great-grandniece of Vincent van Gogh and herself a renowned botanical artist) he inherited his artistic talent. When he goes on walkabouts in the African wilds it is not with a bag of salt and penknife in his rucksack, but pencil and sketchbook.

I am now the proud owner of five beautiful works by Bowen Boshier. You can see his spellbinding art on his website.

David Livingstone – The Man Who Smoked and Thundered

The famous missionary and explorer who wouldn't go any further

DAVID LIVINGSTONE IS arguably the most famous missionary of all time. He led numerous expeditions into the dark African interior, ostensibly to make and save Christian souls. However, in all his travels he made only one conversion, a man who eventually backslid.

Although he fought tirelessly to end the heinous business of slavery in south-central Africa, he is remembered more as an explorer and most notably the one who discovered the largest waterfall on the continent. Like most of the explorers in Africa during Victorian times (Burton and Speke, Mungo Park, Henry Morton Stanley, Candido José da Costa Cardoso and many more), Livingstone was really after the grand prize of the day – locating the source of the Nile.

As much as he was a failure as a missionary, the good Scottish doctor was a superb naturalist. He was never in the class of a Darwin or a Humboldt, but the observations he recorded are insightful and copious. From his first step into the wild, Livingstone kept meticulous notes, as though he knew he was destined for greatness and, although he loved preaching and decrying the evils of the slave trade that was pervasive across the region at the time, he was clearly far more interested in exploration and the natural environment than he was in saving souls.

The pages of his diaries are filled with notes of amazing beasts, including the incident in which he was attacked and severely injured by a lion. There are notes on birds of wondrous shape and shade he saw, insects and plants.

The mangosteen tree – ngobendlovu in a local lingo, the tree that even an elephant cannot bend due to its reputed erectile effect on men – was named in his honour, *Garcinia livingstonii*. Pious, teetotalling and abstemious as he might have been in other ways, the missionary was known to have had a robust desire for the indigenous women he encountered on his travels.

On matters geographical and hydrological he lavished equal attention. He was the first person to note the capricious and seemingly illogical nature of the various channels flowing in and out of the Okavango Delta. Following what he calls the Teoughe and Tamunak'le Rivers (probably the Boteti and Thamalakane) he reflects: "Being essentially the same river, they can never outrun each other. If either could ... we then have the phenomenon of a river flowing two ways, but this has never been observed to take place and it is doubtful it can ever occur in this locality."

The enigmatic waterways of this area had posed a perplexing hydrological puzzle to people over the ages and continued to do so until quite recently. He was right in one respect: that a river cannot defy gravity. There are, however, other forces that can and in the 1980s the tectonic fractures, which underpin the Kalahari sand basin, were identified as warping the surface from time to time.

Given all that we know about him, it seems an historical anachronism to discover that, contrary to the popular mythology of the man, we find that the closer he drew to the mighty falls he was to name, the more we see him acting like a stubborn mule that just will not be coaxed any further.

Why did David Livingstone, one of the most famous explorers of all time, not want to see the waterfall he was to immortalise and that would in turn immortalise him? If you had been with him at the time you might have thought he was trying his damnedest to avoid them.

Also curious is the fact that in all his wanderings, in naming Victoria Falls it was the only time that in his diaries and on his maps, this champion of Africa and African peoples did not use the existing local name. Instead he chose to name the falls after the ruler of the most powerful empire the world has seen.

Is it possible that – it's my thesis at any rate – it was because he had his eye on an even grander prize: not content with the "doctor" that prefixed his name, he yearned for the touch of the silver blade to his shoulder that would confer a regal "sir" to his low-born title? It might well go to his humble beginnings in a mill town in damp Scotland.

David Livingstone was born into poverty in Blantyre in 1813. The family lived in a tenement building for workers of a cotton factory next to the River Clyde. At the age of ten he was sent to work in the mill of Henry Monteith & Co. The factory stood under the iron suspension bridge on Station Road where a museum to the mill's most famous son now stands.

David and his brothers worked fourteen-hour shifts as piercers, tying broken cotton threads to the looms. By saving his earnings and by balancing books while working he was able to educate himself well enough to attend Anderson's College in nearby Glasgow (now the University of Strathclyde). From there he went on to what is now the Royal College of Physicians and Surgeons of Glasgow.

There he was deemed "worthy but remote from brilliant": something like getting the progress prize at school these days. Yet still he managed to gain a scholarship to study further in London. There he was swept up in the anti-slavery movement and joined the London Mission Society (LMS). In 1841 they sent him south to help carry the torch of Christianity and Empire into the furthest corners of southern Africa.

The LMS had set up mission stations mainly in the area north of the Orange River to minister to the Khoi, Griquas and Tswana peoples there, led by very capable men such as Moffat, Campbell, Douglas and Philip. The young Scottish preacher delivered his first sermon in a tiny church at a place that is now shown on maps as Campbell. Just what the locals made of this broad Lanarkshire brogue one can only guess. You can imagine them going home and telling their children, "white guy says blessed are the cheese makers!"

History tells us the young preacher was so traumatised by the experience he fled to the safe haven of his host in South Africa, John Moffat. The older missionary and his wife Mary had founded the Kuruman Mission where he preached to the Bechuana and Khoi people and where he famously translated the Bible into Tswana.

Three years later David married their oldest child, a daughter also named Mary. Being the wife of an explorer proved increasingly arduous for Mary and she bounced between Kuruman, Griquatown, England and Scotland, as well as accompanying her husband on various expeditions. Two of their six children were born on the road.

In 1852 she and her children accompanied their relentless father across the Kalahari's punishing sand expanse. The group decamped on the shores of Lake Ngami, then a brimming fount of plenty amid the scorching sands. Livingstone left his family there and went off on foot with a small entourage to see where those waters might lead.

While Livingstone went on his adventures, Mary and her children contracted fevers. Two-month-old Elizabeth did not have the strength to survive the persistent attacks and finally she succumbed. In those days it was thought that malaria was caused by bad air surrounding steamy bodies of water, hence *mal aria*. At times mother and children were reduced to eating locusts to survive.

Mary's mother had been right when she warned her daughter of the perils that would confront her by marrying the impetuous Scotsman. It is hardly surprising that we find her taking to the bottle for solace and she is reputed to have become an alcoholic.

Her husband, on the other hand, was a strict teetotaler and on expeditions he would not permit spirits nor even sugar or jam to be included on the expedition shopping lists. Not even tea, kin ye hawp it! He expected his European companions to follow his own abstemious ways as well as "going native" in eating habits. He modeled his own diet and lifestyle on that of the Africans he met and with whom he ventured. They in turn adored and even idolised him.

On the Zambezi expeditions which followed his "discovery" of Victoria Falls, Livingstone had numerous sharp conflicts with his crew. He was quick to criticise, blame and fire people. He dismissed the famous artist and fellow explorer Thomas Baines on grounds of thievery; charges Baines vehemently denied. More than once he drove people crazy with anger.

To his fellow expedition members he lacked what today we would call good people skills. They used words including ruthless, authoritarian, secretive, spiteful, vindictive, jealous, deceitful and even double-dealing. They characterised him as being secretive, self-righteous and moody, someone who could not tolerate criticism.

Expedition physician John Kirk wrote of the Zambezi expedition of 1858: "I can come to no other conclusion than that Dr. Livingstone is out of his mind and a most unsafe leader."

The very least we can say about him was that he was single-minded; on a mission you might say. Some months after leaving Mary with their children at Lake Ngami in late 1852, we find him entering the domain of Chief Sebituane of the Makololo tribe along the Chobe River. Here, in the company of hunter William Oswell, he made camp and seemed to stall unnecessarily, even when the African chief told him of a great waterfall downriver, which he notes in his diary as *mo ku sa tunya musi* – "where there is always smoke rising".

It is highly likely that the cause of Livingstone's delay was his receiving dispatches from another traveller, the Portuguese hunter-trader Antonio da Silva Porto. From somewhere near the falls Porto sent Livingstone not only his regards but also a hamper containing preserved fruit, fresh bread, cabbages and two wheels of Dutch cheese.

Livingstone did not acknowledge either the kindness nor accept an invitation to visit the ivory trader's camp. In his diary he denigrates the friendly Portuguese trader as a half-caste traveller and then only in passing. The famously indefatigable Scottish explorer was notoriously parsimonious, even by Scottish standards. He might well have been offended by such ostentatious shows of luxury, but also he might have had darker motives.

Then, to compound matters, he received an invitation from another explorer, László Magyar. The Hungarian was waiting near the falls while hoping for an invitation to visit Livingstone's camp upstream that never came. Imagine, a huge geographical prize so close, possibly never seen before by a European, and not one but three of them converge on the place at the very same time.

In fact Porto had been traversing the area for some years and would have been familiar with the falls that today we know as Mosi-au-Tunya, the smoke that thunders (that now-famous plume has recently been accorded its own cloud type classification, *cumulus var. caractagenitus*).

But even Porto and Magyar were not the strongest claimants to being the first Europeans to see the falls. A strong contender is the hunter Henry Hartley. His family claimed they had heard a story from Hartley's gun-bearer, Cresjan, in which he recalled them visiting a great cataract with rainbows and drenching spray in 1848. There is no other in the region that matches the description.

There are also stories of Boer hunters, people who did not write at all, having reached the Zambezi at least a decade before, but even that is just an historical footnote. For centuries before Europeans arrived in the area, Arab ivory and slave traders had been plying the Zambezi and in fact all the large rivers of Africa that flow into the Indian Ocean.

Of one thing we can be certain: Livingstone was not the first person to see Victoria Falls. He was not even the first European person to gaze upon the largest waterfall in Africa, nor were the Arabs. Batoka or Tonga people had been living in the area for many centuries and they must have noticed a great chasm capturing the wide river, as well as the billowing fountain that from time to time would have sprayed over them. There have even been archaeological finds in the area suggesting it was inhabited from the time of our ancestors, *Homo habilis*.

As things turn out Livingstone was a remarkable man but he was also a shameless self-promoter. All he had to do was ignore the fact that anyone else who could write in English had ever seen the falls before him. And so, when the other two Europeans in the area left,

Livingstone finally did approach the falls and he made up a version of history that suited him.

By and by we find him finally making his way down the Zambezi, from its confluence with the Chobe, in the company of Makololo polers. As he came in sight of the famous spray it would have been in full spate with the plume visible from as far as about fifty kilometres.

Sustained summer storms along the Zambezi River's upper course in Barotseland swell the river so that when its waters reach Victoria Falls an average of six thousand cubic metres (or tonnes) of water cascade over a one thousand five hundred metre long gorge every second, creating the widest curtain of falling water on our planet. By way of comparison, the Victoria Falls is twice as high as the Niagara and about one third more than the Iguazu Falls.

On 16 November his polers were guiding him in their mokoro canoe through a maze of braided channels between sylvan islands towards the great column of spray: "At one time we seemed to be going right into the gulf, but though I felt a little tremor, I said nothing, believing I could face the difficulty as well as my guides."

They landed on an island right on the edge of the abyss with a double rainbow arching over the gorge where they were drenched in the billowing spray. Livingstone crawled to the very edge and peered into the squall. What he imagined he saw only he could say; maybe it was the fabled Nyaminyami serpent that is reputed to live there, who knows? What he did not see were any angels weeping.

The account of a scene "so lovely they must have been gazed upon by angels in their flight" came only later, when the man was back in the United Kingdom and busily building his own legend. What he did write at the time was somewhat more prosaic: "No one can imagine the beauty of this view from anything witnessed in England."

Livingstone returned to Britain to raise funds and visit his family: Mary had scooped up what remained of them and sought shelter with friends of her husband. Wherever he went he was feted by all and was certainly at that time the most famous man in the British Empire.

People were thrilled by the explorer's accounts of his travels and were surprised to learn that the African interior was not all arid deserts but was instead filled with forests, rivers and fertile plains.

This helped greatly in promoting the idea of an expedition to navigate the Zambezi River from the coast.

The celebrated explorer had got a taste of grandeur and this seems to have inflamed a dream – to use the river as a shipping highway. He sold the idea of the Batoka Plains becoming a profitable source of cotton, food and other commodity crops that would replace slavery as the main commercial enterprise of the region.

His main sponsors, still the LMS, did not seem to mind much that he had failed miserably in his primary task of converting African heathens to Christianity. Opening up the African hinterland as a new sphere for British influence and trade, on the other hand, was real man's work, and where Empire went Christianity was sure to follow.

In 1858 Livingstone began to assemble a team that would meet at the mouth of the Zambezi River where they would await the arrival of a steamboat specifically designed to navigate the mighty river. In early 1862 his wife Mary arrived on the boat, but her days were already numbered. She was greatly weakened by continued exposure to malaria. On top of that she had become entirely dependent on strong spirits to soothe body, mind and soul. Her husband must have known this, but it did not seem to diminish his fondness for her.

The brave band ventured upriver but once again Mary succumbed to the dreaded "bad air". She died on 27 April 1862 and was buried on the north bank of the river at Chupanga. That was a terrible blow to the explorer but another was shortly to follow.

Chupanga was only about one third of the distance to their eventual turn-around point but from there things began to fall apart between the leader, Baines, Kirk and the rest of the team, as we have already heard. Livingstone became increasingly grim and uncommunicative, often turning on his colleagues with petty and vindictive accusations. He expected them to share his own well-documented (by him) super-human powers of endurance. He displayed a very un-Christianlike lack of sympathy, even when they fell ill.

Having previously travelled mostly with Africans, he found it increasingly testing to get along with and "nanny" the other Europeans. They probably spent their days on board smoking and playing cards, and probably drinking on the sly. When they reached Cahora Bassa they were confronted by a narrowing gorge, rapids in front and a series of cataracts receding beyond.

They tried to take a detour up the Ruvuma tributary but the paddle of their steam boat got so fouled and broken by the bodies of dead slaves dumped into the river by slave traders, it marked the end of the watery road for the expedition. Mary was only newly dead and now his dreams of fame and riches were in tatters. He was bankrupt and in deep debt.

But, true to his declaration that "I am prepared to go anywhere, so long as it is forward", January 1866 sees him back in Africa, this time openly searching for the source of the Nile. Unfortunately he aimed too far south, but in doing so saw many amazing things and had some very big adventures, not all of them good ones.

By August he had reached Lake Malawi, but by this stage most of his supplies, including all his medicines, had been stolen. He was suffering from cholera and tropical ulcers and had to rely on Arab slave traders for food and shelter. They would have him eat in a roped-off enclosure for the entertainment of locals in return for his food.

By July 1771 he was following the Lualaba River, a tributary of the Congo, which he wrongly hoped would lead him to the Nile. At Nyangwe he witnessed several hundred slaves being massacred by slavers. This so shattered him he abandoned any more dreams of adventure and struggled back to Lake Tanganyika, reaching Ujiji after a four hundred kilometre slog.

This point in his life marks the change from eager and energetic explorer to increasingly desperate man on the run. When newspaper reporter HM Stanley met him at Ujiji on the shores of Lake Tanganyika in 1871 he found Livingstone to be nearly blind from dust, crippled by dysentery and with flesh-eating bugs burrowing beneath his skin.

Trudging for years through thick sand and mud had brought ghastly ulcers to his feet and legs. Muscle, tendon and even bone of his previously "hard as a board" limbs were being eaten away. Severe dysentery had led to bleeding haemorrhoids. Numerous bouts of malaria (the dreaded black-water fever) had weakened his kidneys and pneumonia wracked his lungs.

The missionary managed to persuade the reporter from the *New York Herald* to keep any information of his physical condition out of his dispatches. Livingstone refused to accompany Stanley back to Britain to seek proper medical care for fear the reality of his pathetic condition would scupper his legacy.

Livingstone made ink from wild berries with which he penned a two-page letter, addressed to a friend, Horace Waller, the man who would later edit and compile his diaries – expunging all the negative content. Stanley delivered the letter in London but its contents remained a secret for more than a hundred and forty years.

Those faded pages lay among Livingstone's papers but were illegible due to the all-but-invisible ink. However, around 2010 a team working at Birkbeck University in London managed, using multi-spectral imaging, to enhance the faded handwriting: "I am terribly knocked up, but this is for your own eye only – in my second childhood [by then he had lost most of his teeth] a dreadful old fogie – doubtful if I live to see you again."

David Livingstone died in May 1873 at the age of sixty in the village of Chief Chitambo near the Bangwelu Swamps in northern Zambia and was buried there under a baobab tree. Black-water fever and acute dysentery had finally whittled away his once formidable body.

My first magazine cover-story assignment was to Victoria Falls. In our hard-knocks school of travel journalism there was one golden rule: come back with the photos, or don't come back. On our return we could concoct any story, but pictures could not be retaken.

I was staying at newly built Tongabezi Lodge, about fifteen kilometres upstream from the falls. I managed to persuade a group of Dutch guests to accompany me in a long aluminium banana boat to the island where the famous Victorian explorer had landed and peered down into raging Batoka Gorge.

Imitating Livingstone I put on a cavalier face but our one-engine craft had me apprehensive. I managed to herd the other sightseers to the spray-drenched edge of what is now known as Livingstone's Island, complete with colourful umbrellas, and then "shot the sherbet out of it" as we used to say. With the falls shoot wrapped, a day or so later I set off on a canoe safari.

In the middle of the wide Zambezi our canoe was hit from beneath by what felt like a ballistic missile. I heard a crash then a crunch as said projectile flung our fragile craft into the air and then sunk its substantial armory into the aft section.

"Swim faster than you have ever swum before," shouted my fellow paddler from Shearwater Adventures. "But don't make a splash or ..." and off he shot for a nearby island like a tiger fish going for a Rapala lure without explaining what he meant.

Lucky for us the hippo began thrashing around our broken boat and gnashing at our equipment, including my camera bag. I managed to hold onto my paddle and reckoned I would not go down without a fight. Approaching the island I noticed a bow wave making towards us and made like a one-bladed paddle steamer.

Aquaman grabbed my hand and hauled me onto dry land and over a conveniently placed fallen log just as the bellowing river monster surged out the water. We were safe, but my cover shot was not. When the Shearwater rescue boat arrived they thought I was crazy when I insisted on returning to the scene of the crime.

"Don't you know," someone repeated the great safari myth, "hippos kill more people than any other animal in Africa!" I knew well enough they didn't (when it comes to vertebrates that honour goes to crocodiles) but I had had close-up experience of how deadly they could be nonetheless. Still, I was determined not to be the first person to break the golden rule.

Those were the good old days of photographic film and I knew that, if undamaged, the little airtight film canisters would float. We managed to scoop up a bunch of them before the irate hippo found us and we had to skedaddle.

In those days we would hold our breaths until our film (always Fuji Velvia 50) came back from the lab and we'd lay the sheets on a light table to check if we had indeed got the shot. The cover image of a group of tourists poking cheerful umbrellas at "the smoke that thunders" remains one of my best.

While relaxing back at Tongabezi I found a copy of Rob

Mackenzie's book, *David Livingstone: The Truth Behind the Legend*. It was there that I met the other Livingstone, the irascible, moody, vindictive, crazy (add whatever adjectives you will) man of whom most of us were not previously aware.

His end was extremely sad, in a lonely place and abandoned by all but three of his once rather grand and loyal African entourage. In spite of all his fame and adoration in Britain, his achievements and sufferings, no "sir" was ever to come his way. He was, however, awarded a gold medal by the Royal Geographical Society and made a member of that august organisation.

Rather than dwelling on his dubious behaviour on the Zambezi steamboat expedition, or his final words in that letter to Horace Wallace, we might consider what others had to say about his legacy. The famous British geologist and explorer JW Gregory believed he made the greatest contribution to African geography ever.

Of Livingstone's 1858–62 expedition, biographer George Martelli wrote: "It was an extraordinary performance of imaginative enterprise, grit and dogged perseverance eclipsing all his other exploits. With all his faults, he towers over ordinary men."

It seems to me to be a fairly universal trait that we are quick to judge others we do not know. Quite often our opinions are moulded by others, such as a biographer who really liked or disliked their subject. How, for example, can we evaluate a man who died more than a century ago? Was David Livingstone a huge success or was he a failure, was he hero or villain?

I prefer to judge him by his own words. The final image of him I like to muse on has him sitting at his portable camp table in a shady spot on the bank of the Zambezi River. It is 1852. He dips his quill into a bottle of Indian ink, dabs the nib and begins to scratch a letter to his beloved Mary: "I never show all my feelings, but I can say truly, my dearest, that I loved you when I married you, and the longer I lived with you, I loved you the better."

In a final analysis maybe we can say he was Scottish: as tough on those around him as he was on himself – except for his African companions on whom he lavished most of his deeper feelings and who in turn virtually worshipped him.

Modjadji – The Rain Queens

*Royal rainmakers, it's demanding work
but the rewards can be great*

SOUTH AFRICA IS, FOR THE MOST PART, a dry land. Even the wettest places, such as the Tsitsikamma and Magoebaskloof forest areas, are susceptible to occasional drought. Since time immemorial, preserved in the rock art of the San people, rain creatures have been central to our mythology. Hardly surprising, therefore, that rainmakers have played an influential role in the affairs of men and deities – or indeed women, as we shall see.

With only a few notable exceptions, we of urban allegiance or European extraction know very little about these mythical figures who were, and in some places still are, pivotal to the wellbeing of people still living close to nature, without access to a reliable municipal water supply. One example is the subject of this story, the Modjadji Rain Queen.

A few examples of rainmakers come to us from the diaries of white folk who lived close to indigenous people and felt at least a modicum of tolerance for their customs. One of the rainmakers we can read about is the Sotho individual Mpunzane Mhowelela. As a boy he would walk about around the country, working his way as far from his Lowveld home as Port Elizabeth.

He began practicing his art at the kraal of his mother in the Bushbuckridge area. Rainmaking is passed down the female line, like mitochondrial DNA. A rainmaker must have drunk from its mother's breasts, goes the lore. Along with her milk the mother passes on the secrets of the magic to her chosen offspring, usually a male. The rainmaker will establish a secret place, usually deep in a dark and forested kloof, where he keeps his magical tools and casts his spells.

The usual course of business is that, when rain is required for planting, a clan will collect a tribute that the headman delivers to the rainmaker in order to secure his services. When the rainmaker accepts the "gift" he tells the headman to return to his kraal and tell his people when to begin planting. If rain holds off there will invariably be a good reason: not everyone contributed to the gift, or some people had started sowing seeds before the rainmaker had consulted with the spirits. Then another gift is required to pacify them.

In times of extreme drought sacrifices might be needed. Usually a goat or two would do, but should things get worse (and invariably they will from time to time) sometimes even cattle would be delivered to the sorcerer. The beasts will be slaughtered and the meat left on a rock near his secret shelter. It should never be eaten, at least not by other humans, but a passing hyena or leopard would relish the easy meal.

In the most extreme of droughts, however, a human sacrifice would be required to appease the angry spirits. There were reports that not all the deaths at Mhowelela's kraal were natural ones (in traditional African culture no death is natural but is invariably the result of malevolent witchcraft or takati).

So far-reaching was the reputation of Mhowelela that once a year a deputation would arrive from the king of Swaziland with a tribute to secure his services. His reputation was vast and, it seems, no one ever dared to question his abilities. If a rain shower fell in only one limited area it was because that chief had paid the rainmaker an extra tribute. You could not argue with the spirits.

The best of rainmakers can become not only extremely influential but rich as well. Invariably they become chiefs. The most powerful clan of rainmakers in South Africa originally came from a land far to the north, arriving in the Limpopo region some centuries ago.

Trouble started in the house of Balebedu in the Kingdom of Monomotapa. The ruler's son impregnated his own sister, Dzugundini, in order for her to gain rainmaking powers. Another version has the king sleeping with her, his daughter, but we'll never know for sure. Whichever way it played out, brother and sister fled Zimbabwe and hotfooted southwards. As with ancient Greece, African folklore is all mythology, part Illiad and part Odyssey.

They settled in the relatively fertile Molototsi valley, northeast of Magoebaskloof. The ruler there was a Chief Mugudo and by and by he married Dzugundini. To appease his people, that the matrilineal dynasty of the rainmaker be continued, Mugudo had to impregnate the oldest daughter of his union with Dzugundini.

Some time around the year 1800 Maselekwane, a direct descendent of Dzugudini, was inducted as the first Rain Queen to rule over the Balebedu people. She called herself Modjadji, or "ruler of the day". From that time to rather recently a Modjadji rain queen has ruled continuously over the Balebedu.

Such were the reputed powers of the Modjadji to control the clouds that people as powerful as Shaka Zulu sought her skills in times of drought. The second Modjadji is reputed to have been the inspiration for the swashbuckling adventure story by H Rider Haggard, *She*.

As can be imagined of not only a traditional African ruler, but also one uniquely gifted with sacred and supernatural powers, the office of the Modjadji is regulated by a plethora of rules and rituals. For example, she who rules the day should not be seen in public but communicates with her people through male councillors.

She may not marry a man but instead has many female "wives". They are selected from each of the major households of the tribe in order to preserve political unity. Her mates, on the other hand, are selected by a royal council. The chosen ones have no official status and are not allowed to live within the royal household.

In November each year the rain queen presides over the main

rainmaking ceremony at her royal compound in Khetlhakone village. The lush gardens that surround the village are held as testimony to the queen's particular powers. Most impressive in the garden is the collection of cycads, reputedly the largest in existence. The largest species is named *Encephalartos modjadji* and these primitive plants rule the garden, some of their pocked trunks looping along the ground like gigantic vegetal dragons.

However, of late there is once more trouble in the house of Balebedu. I visited the Modjadjiskloof, as the region is now called, in 2004 on assignment to photograph the amazing cycad garden. I took a chance and requested an audience with the newly crowned queen and, completely unexpectedly, it was granted.

More surprisingly, it turned out, because Modjadji VI, Makopo Constance, was extremely unwell at the time. She died within the year of unknown – or at least undisclosed – causes. Rumours flew around like hail stones and along with talk of pneumonia and meningitis, the dreaded HIV was mentioned.

Makobo Constance had been the first in her line to receive a formal education and grew up to be a woman fully in sync with the modern world. She flouted many of the old rules, taking a mate of her own choosing whom she invited to live with her in her royal compound. Many of her subjects, her many tiers of advisers and perhaps the spirits themselves, were not amused.

When Makobo Caroline died on 12 June 2005 her daughter, Masalanabo Caroline, was a three-month-old infant. When it came time to appoint a seventh rain queen things in Modjadji land got interesting in a Shakespearean kind of way.

The land of Modjadji had been divided by the behaviour of Makobo Constance. Some favoured the line of her brother Prince Mpapatla, who had a daughter of his own with his cousin. For the more traditionalists of the tribe the prince's daughter (conceived in the traditional way) was the preferred successor in the Modjadji dynasty.

Uncle Mpapatla was elected as regent of young Princess Masalanabo Caroline until her coming of age in 2021. Who knew what would transpire until then? That was when the state's big guns stepped in. It turned out Queen Makobo VI had been progressive in political as well as social spheres, having gained the favour of successive presidents.

In order to stave off insurrection at the Balebedu royal kraal, the princess was shipped down to Johannesburg (by sanction of the Traditional Leadership and Governance Framework Act) to live with a government-appointed guardian. The person chosen was Mathole Motshekga, a member of the Balebedu clan and husband of the more famous Angie, one of the ANC's inner circle.

In the meantime the levers of climatic control in Modjadjiskloof remain firmly in the hands of the rain gods.

Dr James Barry – The Doctor Who Wasn't

The Cape's most extraordinary military medical officer

WHO DOES NOT KNOW THE STORY of Doctor James Barry, one of the two most famous surgeons to ever practice in South Africa? Both were exceptional in their field and both mixed in the most exulted company. One was a man (Barnard), the other (Barry) was not.

Even on her death, when her real gender was exposed, her true identity was not known for sure until only a few years ago. Much had been written about her in the meantime, a good deal very fanciful for sure. As you can imagine, the revelation caused no end of scandal with statements of "of course I knew" and much amateur psychoanalysing.

One of the first people to properly investigate her life was that great man of South African letters, Lawrence G Green, but he had access to only references from the Cape. I have been a collector of Green's books for many years and my early knowledge of the woman doctor came from his work *Grow Lovely, Growing Old: The Story of Cape Town's Three Centuries.*

Green uncovered a lot and sniffed out quite a bit of the truth, scanning the official archives, scouring Cape Town's libraries and old newspapers and interviewing as many people as he could find who had links to the famous man-impersonating army doctor. One problem was that Barry concealed as much as she could and another was that her behaviour caused others to conjecture much about her that was way off the mark.

Two things about Barry were evident to anyone who interacted with her: the first was that she was tiny, with a high pitched voice and without any facial hair, and that she seemed to be protected from on high. This was often necessary, for Barry was quick to insult anyone, including those in high office and even get into fights.

While studying medicine at Edinburgh she briefly took up boxing but it was noted that she always seemed to be protecting her chest and not her head. So she took up fencing where she acquitted herself excellently. When she joined the army as a junior medical officer she began to wear an overly large dragoon's sword. Insults and threats led to duels on more than one occasion.

The most famously documented was her pistol duel with a Captain Josias Cloete of the 21st Light Dragoons. It was triggered when Cloete told Barry she rode more like a women than a man and she whacked him across the face with her riding crop. Barry proved to be not only an accomplished swordswomen but also the more accurate shot. Cloete's shot went wide while Barry's knocked off the captain's tall, cylindrical dragoon's cap.

A later posting sent Barry to the Crimea as Deputy Inspector-General of hospitals. While mounted imperiously on horseback, Barry halted none other than the exulted Florence Nightingale in front of a hospital and, for reasons not fully known, gave her a real tongue-lashing in front of a large crowd. Later the famous nurse wrote: "I never had such a blackguard rating in all my life – I who have had more than any woman … I should say that [Barry] was the most hardened creature I ever met."

It is now known that Barry was born in 1795, ostensibly female. She enrolled at Edinburgh University's celebrated medical school at age fourteen and graduated at seventeen. However, some of her tutors, suspecting she was a pre-pubescent boy, tried to stop her from taking her final exams.

From there she progressed to the United Hospitals of Guy's and St Thomas's where she successfully passed the Royal College of Surgeons of England examination a year later at the age of just eighteen.

Green writes that she served in the Napoleonic Wars in Spain and that she was "probably" at Waterloo. Recent biographers dispute this. We do know that she joined the army as a hospital assistant and in 1816 was posted to the Cape as an assistant surgeon (the rank equal to that of lieutenant). Just about from the time of her arrival it became evident that she had protection from above, which turned out to be no less than the "close to king and god" governor, Lord Charles Somerset.

This led to the belief that she had been high born. Green conjectured that she was the daughter of the Scottish aristocrat the Earl of Buchan. Others thought she might be the illegitimate child of the Duke of York, second son of King George III, sent to the colonies as were so many black sheep and illegitimate offspring of families back then. As it turns out, she was none of these.

She was just five foot in height and she had three-inch heels fitted to her riding boots. She also wore an obviously heavily padded jacket. The coloured folk of Cape Town, always quick of wit, nicknamed her the "kapok dokter" – the cotton-wool doctor.

Apart from the run-of-the-mill social insults, Barry also gained enemies by criticising local officials in their handling of medical matters, but each time, apart from being right and holding the moral high ground, her close relationship with the governor meant that the repercussions of her outspoken views were usually smoothed over. She was concerned with things like humane care for hospital patients and basic rights such as medical care for prisoners, which were not high priorities at the time.

Just a few years later she was spectacularly promoted to the post of Colonial Medical Officer, giving her sweeping medical powers and responsibilities throughout the Cape Colony. She almost immediately went about offending others in positions of power but, as we shall see, most often for very good reason.

According to Green's research, many patients remembered Barry with appreciativeness and mentioned her kind bedside manner. One patient at Wynberg military hospital is recorded as saying: "No man could show such sympathy with one in pain." Whether or not she had guessed the doctor's subterfuge is not noted.

Others had much more cause for gratitude and none more so than Jacob Elliot who she found in Cape Town's infamous "tronk". His thigh was fractured but he had been left without any medical care, no crutches, no bed let alone blanket or pillow and in great pain and misery. The doctor was informed he had been given water only once in the previous two days.

Barry publically denounced the prison authorities, who in turn summonsed her in front of the Fiscal Commission to answer charges of slander. Barry refused to answer their accusations and instead threatened: "If I had my sword when Mr Fiscal proposed sending me to the tronk, I should certainly have cut off both his ears!" The upshot was that they in turn ended up having to dance in front of the governor and prison reforms were soon implemented.

While inspecting the lunatics' ward at Somerset Hospital she noted: "The whole establishment appears devoid of cleanliness, order or professional care." She found three or more of the inmates to be perfectly sane. None of them had even the slightest of comforts. She also spared a thought for the sentries on duty who were given no shelter in any weather. Needless to say, improvements were quickly made, one of which was that windows be opened and fresh air let in, going against the best medical advice of the time.

Her next crusade took her into the Overberg, up the valley of Hemel-en-Aarde, heaven and earth. Except she found that it was anything but heaven for the inmates at the leper hospital there. "Nothing could exceed the misery of the lepers. Their clothing was dirty and bad, the food scanty and ill-managed. These miserable people were confined to a small space of the really beautiful and ample land allotted to them. The hospital was squalid and wretched beyond description."

Once again reforms were quick to follow. Barry ordered the implementation of a military-standard diet regime including the regular supply of milk, rice, coffee, vegetables, bread and meat. She was herself a strict vegetarian and drank only modest amounts of champagne on official occasions.

This was all quite revolutionary at the time, but her most lasting medical legacy is that she is thought to have performed the first known caesarian section operation at the Cape – at any rate the first one where both mother and child survived. This has long been hotly contested and even Green writes that "Barry was a physician" and "I cannot find a scrap of evidence that she ever practiced major surgery."

The doctor's most thorough biographer, HM du Preez, however, is quite sure about it, noting that while studying in London Barry had been instructed by some of the most prominent surgeons of the day.

Caesarian or not, a healthy baby was delivered and named James Barry Munnik. By and by the names were handed down the generations and it was with some surprise that South African Prime Minister between the world wars, General JB Hertzog, learned from whence came his own name. When he learned of the doctor's gender bending ways, however, he was less than impressed, so the story goes.

One day Dr Barry was summoned by a clergyman to pull an aching tooth. Not for the first time she flew off the high-pitched handle, insisting she was not a mere tooth puller. Typical of her wayward behaviour she sent a farrier over with instructions to pull the tooth of the priest's donkey. A complaint to Lord Charles Somerset was deflected with a "no one pays attention to what Barry says".

It turns out Barry's closeness to the governor was established soon after her arrival at Table Bay. Among her first patients were Somerset's extremely ill daughter and the wife of Admiral Jaleel Brenton who was close to death. Both experienced remarkable recoveries.

To visiting Lord Albermarle, Somerset described Barry as "one of the most skillful of physicians and the most wayward of men". Albermarle insisted on being seated next to Barry at an official dinner, later describing this "beardless lad" as having "a certain effeminacy in his manner which he seemed to be always striving to overcome".

He goes on to say of Barry: "A mystery attached to Doctor Barry's whole professional career. Quarrelsome and frequently guilty of flagrant breaches of discipline, he was sent home several times under arrest. His offences were always condoned at headquarters."

Rumours about the close relationship between the governor and the doctor began to circulate. In June 1824 a poster was pasted in town declaring the writer had "detected Lord Charles buggering Dr Barry …." This was an extremely dangerous accusation to make against a governor, partly because at that time homosexuality was illegal and carried strenuous punishment, and also because if the governor found out who you were you would be unlikely to see sunshine again.

It has been suggested that Somerset discovered Barry's secret early on and that they did enjoy a physical relationship. No sexual relationship, either way, was ever revealed.

Following an illustrious and colourful career at the Cape, Barry was posted to Mauritius, Jamaica, St Helena, Corfu and Canada, insulting people left and right as she went. On St Helena she was court martialled for "conduct unbecoming of the character of an Officer and a Gentleman". She was found not guilty. Did Lord Somerset's influence reach that far, one wonders.

The truth about Barry is less exalted as many surmised and, because of it, all the more remarkable. Had she indeed been the daughter of an earl or a prince, her eccentric career decision and behaviour might more easily be understood as typical of the haughtiness and nuttiness associated with the aristocracy.

She was in fact born Margaret Anne Bulkley in Ireland in 1795, the child of a Catholic couple, Mary-Ann and Jeremiah Bulkley who ran a weighing house in County Cork. His Catholic ways lost Jeremiah his weigh house licence but seems to have endeared him to the Irish Catholic nationalists of the day.

That must have been how people such as the Earl of Buchan (once thought of as the most likely candidate for her father) came to sponsor her medical studies, first in Scotland and thereafter in England. It was also an introduction from Earl Buchan, a Scottish supporter of the Catholic cause, that led her directly into the drawing room and thereafter the bedrooms (for purely medical reasons, mind) of Lord Somerset at the Cape.

On 30 November 1789, Margaret Ann Bulkley boarded a ketch-rigged fishing boat for Scotland. That was also the day Margaret Ann disappeared and into her shoes stepped James Barry, but why?

Lawrence G Green's best summation is that it was in order that she could follow a love interest who was an army medical officer. "This is one of the points on which all previous investigators are agreed," he writes. He even has a name, Sir Andrew Smith KCB, stating they were both Scots and of about the same age. But of course Margaret, or James, was not Scottish.

I doubt very much that, as a lowly medical officer, she would have had the influence to dictate where or how she followed a fellow – at the time junior – army medical officer around the world. In time Barry rose to the rank of Inspector General in charge of military hospitals, the second highest rank for a medical officer in the British Army. This was most likely due to her own effective medical ideas rather than any outside influence, which would have run dry once she left the Cape.

It would have been far easier to follow the officer as a simple civilian. Civilian family and military groupies were known to follow the British Army around the world, setting up marquees at battlegrounds, on the high ground whenever possible, to get a good view of the action. A kind of early incarnation of the "barmy army".

Nevertheless, the debate has not abated over the course of two hundred years. There have been numerous biographies written, papers debating her sexuality published and so forth. Was she female, male, cross-gender, transgender; there are so many groups recognised these days that we maybe need to think of a gender continuum instead of discrete categories.

When Barry died of dysentery in 1865 the truth was discovered by the cleaner who prepared her body for burial. The woman wanted money, but Barry's physician who had stated "male" on the death certificate refused. The wily scrubber women took her story to the press.

In typical military response to the scandal, the British Army sealed all her records for a hundred years. When they were released in the 1950s the story of the lady army physician who pretended to be a man was reawakened with renewed fascination. There has been a play written about her, *Whistling Psyche* by Sebastian Barry, and a song by contemporary folk duo Gilmore & Roberts entitled "Doctor James".

In 2016 a rigorously researched biography published in England provided all the substance to the body of the story, except for only one bit that really counts: was Margaret Anne Bulkley female or male, heterosexual or homosexual, or was she somewhere else along the gender continuum?

At the time of writing there was a debate about whether overly masculine female athletes should be given hormones to counterbalance their high testosterone levels to level the race track (should feminine male athletes be similarly boosted?).

These were not debates that were considered polite, or even legal, back in Dr Barry's time. Even today you cannot have this discussion in many places, but it is a fact of the human condition and when we manage to get every aspect of human sexuality out into the open, it will already be too late.

I'm a fan of detective stories and am inclined to fall back on one of the fundamental laws of crime busting: start with the obvious. That is why I'd wager she was simply a female born into a man's world who wanted more.

Eugène Marais – The Ant Man of the Waterberg

Seeing worlds among grains of sand

EUGÈNE MARAIS, PRODIGY, POLYMATH and junkie is best remembered for his writings about baboons. However, I believe it is a lesser-known work that – in my opinion at any rate – more truly reveals his genius.

Eugène Nielen Marais was both a reader and a writer. He was born in Pretoria in the year the dusty Voortrekker town was founded, 1872. His first professional job was as parliamentary reporter for the *Volksblad* newspaper. He was such a caustic critic of verkrampte president Paul Kruger's cronies he was tried for high treason and barred from the volksraad, or parliament.

In his early twenties Marais was one of the town dandies, complete with boater hat, bowtie, silver-tipped cane and a predilection for taking a fashionable amount of morphine. As editor of *Land en Volk* he championed the new language of Afrikaans and used it to write most of his journalistic, naturalistic and poetic works.

Being one of the fledgling Transvaal republic's brightest stars, he was sent to study law at Edinburgh, which he found to be tedious and so spent most of his time in the tartan town attending much more stimulating medical lectures. It was a time when the radical ideas of Freud and Darwin were swirling around. He did finally graduate with a law degree and returned to the Transvaal.

In 1893 he met Aletta Beyers of Durban and wrote to a friend that she was "the most perfect female in body and mind that God ever planted in South Africa". Looking at the old photographs of Lettie Beyers (as she was called) it is easy to concur with the lovelorn young man. They were married in 1894 and Lettie soon became pregnant. On a frigid evening on 8 July 1895 her waters broke.

On the day Pretoria was busy celebrating the official opening of the Delagoa railway line. A doctor Kriel was summoned but arrived only in the early hours of the morning, bolstered by much bonhomie and mampoer. A baby boy was delivered as dawn cracked the sky. Both mother and baby, also named Eugène, seemed to be healthy and happy.

However, a few days later Lettie came down with a fever. Within a week she fell into a coma. It turned out the doctor had not sterilised his instruments properly and septicaemia led to puerperal fever. She died on the 17th of that month. Marais never got over this loss and from then until his dying day – he committed suicide with a shotgun to the head in 1936 on the farm Pelindaba in the Magaliesberg – he turned increasingly to morphine to dull the pain.

All his life Marais surrounded himself with insects, reptiles and mammals of many kinds and that is likely what kept him sane in his grief. There was nothing about the natural world that did not excite him. It is frequently noted that genius is only ten per cent inspiration and ninety per cent perspiration. In the case of South Africa's, perhaps, greatest genius it was more like fifty/fifty.

During the Anglo-Boer War he ran arms and ammunition to the Boers by way of Mozambique. With the war over he sank deeper and deeper into depression, dismayed at the cruelty of humans and the suffering of his Afrikaner people. He moved to a remote farm in the Waterberg district and acted as a Justice of the Peace in order to help the poverty-stricken folk there.

That was also where he conducted his observations and experiments with baboons that led to his most famous work, *The Soul of the Ape*. Marais always had an outsider view of things. He reckoned that if the human body was descended from earlier ape-like ancestors, it followed that the human psyche must be similarly evolved. He spent years observing baboon behaviour and also delved into human psychology. He hypnotised people (mainly young women who he found to be most susceptible) in attempts to plumb the primal subconscious.

Marais continued his studying on Oom Gys van Rooyen's farm in Rietfontein where he spent ten years observing termites. At that time they were incorrectly called white ants, the scourge of any timber structure as baboons were to crops (possibly Marais identified with these insect "outsiders" as much as he did with the primates). "Termites (are) in every respect just as wonderful and interesting as anything that has been discovered in South America," he wrote at a time when the world was abuzz with discoveries from the Amazon. "Such observations reveal new wonders every day."

In an old farmhouse that was being devoured from the inside out, the reclusive naturalist discovered a termite nest under the floorboards that was easy to access. Working at night with candles so as not to disturb them unduly, he unlocked many windows and doors into the secret life of termites, insects that are among the Earth's most ancient creatures. Not least of all his observations was how the termitary seemed to have a collective psyche (of course he would think so!).

At the time of Marais's termite observations, drought was squeezing the life out of the Waterberg. No water could be found as far as fifteen metres down the well on Rietfontein farm, and yet in a termitary close by Marais found moist fungus gardens just two metres underground. The fungus gardens were another thing he discovered. Marais enlisted Oom Gys to help him solve the mystery of the termite's water supply.

They dug a hole among a grove of still green wild olive trees on the farm and ten metres down struck water. They also found a tiny horizontal shaft leading sideways to a termite nest some distance away. At another location they found termites digging down more than thirty metres to reach water.

"It was at night, when the rest of nature was quietest, that the fierceness of the fight (the battle for survival of the colony) gained most frenzy," he wrote. He could hear the faint but unceasing alarm calls of the termite soldiers as they battled their deadliest foes, ants. "It aroused in me a feeling of terrible anxiety."

Marais daubed the different classes of termites with contrasting dyes in order to see what they got up to. In doing so he discovered the surprising roles carried out in various areas of the colony by the different groups. On reflection, his deepest perception was that each termitary colony was a unique and discreet organism.

The outside shells we see scattered across the African veld are made from individual grains of sand mixed with termite saliva which, when set, are as hard as concrete. Deep underground, at the centre of each termite mound is a hard brain casing with a brain inside (the queen, or sometimes multiple queens).

The colony took in nutrients from the outside (grass) and processed them in fungal gardens (the stomach of the organism) in order to render the hard cellulose into an edible sugar-based form. Soldier termites were the blood, fighting outside infections and repairing the outer skin wherever it had been rent. The only thing the termite colony could not do (at least not by human standards) was to move about at will.

Between 1925 and '26 Marais wrote his findings in a series of articles in Afrikaans for *Huisgenoot* magazine. In 1927 a book entitled *Vie des Termites* (Life of Termites) appeared in Europe, as if out of the blue. It was written in French by celebrated author Maurice Maeterlinck who had won a Nobel Prize in Literature for make-believe plays such as *l'Ouiseau Bleu* (The Bluebird).

The book appeared to be based largely on, but not credited to, Marais's observations. But how could a noted European man of letters ever have come across the work of a little-known naturalist, labouring in a cultural backwater and writing in an obscure new language? Maeterlinck was not French but Belgian. And, as it turns out, Afrikaans – or the "kitchen Dutch" of the old Cape – is hardly distinguishable from the Flemish spoken in Belgium.

By then Marais, once a firebrand editor as well as a lawyer, had lost his fighting spirit and did not pursue the matter. He died nine years later, his body and soul broken by thirty years of grief, depression and addiction. His good friend Gustav Preller noted that by the end of his life Marais was taking doses of morphine large enough to kill a horse outright.

His poem *Winternag*, published in 1910, helped usher in Afrikaans as a new and mature language. Still today the poem is considered the language's high point.

Many people consider Marais's poetry to be his most lasting and sublime legacy.

As much as I love poetry, and particularly Afrikaans verse, I am not among those who values Marais's poetry over his other achievements. His own book on termites was published a year after his death. It is a work of astonishing rigour and insight and far, far outweighs Maeterlinck's more patchy and fanciful work.

Some people are wont to claim that a book or even a movie changed their lives. You know that it's probably not true and what they actually mean is that either they really liked it or that it is dovetailed neatly with their own perspective on things. So it is with some sense of humiliation that I admit the trajectory of my own life was inexorably altered by this singular work of genius.

At the age of around ten or so I had a medical condition that saw me laid up for much of the summer vacation. The tedium of being confined to the house and watching my older brothers playing outside was largely alleviated by books. Our house was filled with them, which came in handy. Whatever our parents lacked in the department of adult supervision, they more than made up for by stocking our house with books of just about every genre.

Following on from the adventures of *The Famous Five* (thank you Enid Blyton) came children's encyclopaedias and *Jock of the Bushveld*. They in turn led me on to the Reader's Digest condensed classics and later all the literary treasures of the universe.

When I did not have my nose in a book I spent most of my school days running around in the veld digging for snakes and shrews or whatever else I could find. There was a period between being in the army and finding a job that I found myself back in my parents' home with time on my hands. From a bookshelf I picked up, almost at random, an unassuming hardcover matt-black book with chunky white lettering on the spine.

On the front cover, in the bottom right corner, was the heavy white outline of a termite. We knew termites well enough growing up in the Highveld. As flying ants they provided a seasonal sport, while for the rest of the year their earthen mounds gave us endless hours of exploration: it was where snakes, shrews and other small creatures liked to hide.

The book was a first edition, published in 1937 by Methuen and Co, London. Its title was (I have it sitting on my desk as I write this) *The Soul of the White Ant,* written by Eugène N Marais. It reopened my eyes to the deeper world of nature.

When people ask me how one becomes a writer I always give the same answer: you have to be a reader first. And what else was I going to be when I grew up but a nature writer? I have a small black book to thank for that.

George Mossop – *Running the Gauntlet*

A life lived to the fullest on the open veld

THE ANGLO-ZULU WAR OF 1879 is remembered almost entirely for two battles. The most famous one was at Isandhlwana where a Zulu impi inflicted a humiliating blow on a rear detachment of Lord Chelmsford's grand imperial army. The second was a follow-up engagement later that day and all that night at Rork's Drift store and field hospital where a rag-tag assortment of reinforcements, storemen, medics and the wounded put up a most heroic defence.

Whether before a battle, or an international rugby game at Ellis Park, the opening lyrics of the Juluka classic "Impi", cool the blood and raise the hair on one's arms.

Impi! Wo' nans impi iyeza.
Obani benanthinta amabubesi?
War! O here comes war.
Who here can touch the lions?
However, the war that followed was no mere two-day event, lasting

some six months with many other battles and skirmishes. At least as bloody and humiliating for the British forces as Isandhlwana was the battle of Hlobane Mountain. George Mossop, a sixteen-year-old British subject of South African birth, was among those who fought there. His recounting of the action, as well as the events in his life that led up to it, is one of South Africa's best least-known sagas.

George Joseph Mossop was born near Durban or what was then Port Natal, in the Colony of Natal in the early 1860s. He spent his youth running barefoot in the veld around Umvoti where he was supposed to be attending the village school.

"Wanderlust was in my blood," he wrote in his memoirs in 1930, using all the scraps he'd written throughout his extraordinarily adventurous life to bolster his memory. In 1875, at the age of fourteen, he left home and set off for the Transvaal where, he understood, the real wilds of Africa could still be found. "I became a product of the veld and the wide spaces to which I still cling, for I have never lived in a town or near one."

In 1937, the year before he died, when he wrote a preface to his notes he admitted he had never been to the cinema or seen a circus, although he had once seen an aeroplane sailing the sky like an eagle, "though no bird ever kicked up such a fiendish row".

His first year of freedom was spent with a party of Boers shooting game for their skins and to make biltong. The Eastern Transvaal Highveld, now Mpumalanga, was the last refuge of the huge herds of game that once covered the entire grassland biome in tens and hundreds of thousands. Before the arrival of white hunters the Highveld would have hosted a wildlife spectacle far exceeding the now more famous Serengeti Plains.

The region was also covered in wetlands where waterfowl gathered in vast flocks, and great numbers of other birds nested in the extensive reed beds. However, one by one the reed beds were burned to convert the land for grazing. The birds moved off, never to return, and neither did most of the wetlands.

When his hunting party reached the main body of the game migration near present-day Ermelo, the Boers made camp without any hint of haste – they had done this many times before. The Good

Lord would provide. Oxen were unyoked, horses knee-haltered, tents pitched, fires made, then coffee and rusks were handed round. The game was on.

Mossop said of the migration: "The scene which met my eyes the next morning is beyond my power to describe. Game, game everywhere, as far as the eye could see – all on the move, grazing."

It seemed to the inexperienced lad that the game appeared not to be moving but that the Earth itself was carrying the vast herd of animals along with it. As he watched he realised that within the great herd were smaller groups of specific species: a herd of some five hundred black wildebeest moved towards the wagons, stopped, wheeled as one with their heads facing the shooting camp, then up went their white tails and off they moved. Then another, several thousand strong.

Next came a group of about two hundred quaggas, which were called "the zebra of the bush veld". Mossop describes them as being taller, of lighter colour and shaggier than their more common brothers. They charged towards the wagons and came to a stop about sixty metres distant, their hooves ploughing into the ground. Their innate inquisitiveness made them easy to shoot and the writer reckoned this was likely the last of their kind to be seen anywhere.

There were also hundreds of thousands each of blesbok and springbok. Mossop was awed, rendered speechless by the scene, but the Boers calmly went about the business of readying for the slaughter as if it were just another day's work, stretching riems between the wagons and poles on which hides and meat would be hung.

What must the country have looked like, Mossop pondered, before the shooting had begun decades earlier? Black wildebeest moved past them at a canter, hour after hour, making speech all but impossible. The men shot and shot and shot until they could shoot no more. At one point he asked the leader of the group, "old man Visagie", if he did not think it wrong to slaughter all the game to the verge of extinction.

"Can you tell me, Mister Heathen," came the stern reply, "what good this game is doing, running wild over the veld? You *dare* to say that the Lord did not know what he was doing when He placed them here. It is a sin to listen to such words. Never use them again in my presence."

A year later, in 1879, the Zulu War flared up so the sixteen-year-old George rode back to Natal to sign up for duty with the Frontier Light Horse (FLH), a rag-tag group of self-equipped colonials that was modeled on the Boer commando system.

Mossop's Bushman companion of the previous year, Gerswent, pleaded with him not to leave. The wrinkled old man said the British had no hope of beating the mighty Zulus. He had seen the British, he said, stripping naked early in the morning in winter and washing in a river. They even put their heads under the water!

The young adventurer's journey to join up with Colonel Wood's column took him on a tortuous route back across the Highveld and down to the Lowveld. He got caught in a storm on the Berg escarpment near Utrecht and he and his Basuto pony, Warrior, had to brave a night of wind and driving rain "camping" – hiding behind a rock until dawn came and the storm let up.

"Although my pony was only a few feet from me, I could not see him, so thick was the darkness, but I knew that he was standing there with his tail to the blast."

Moans and groans seemed to grip the mountainside, rushing sounds becoming ever louder until they seemed to be upon the miserable young man. When a reedbuck appeared out of the squall and let out a shrill whistle, the man crawled up close to his pony for comfort. In his day people did not prepare *padkos* but took whatever they had to hand. Then it was usually just a strip of biltong. Mossop finished his while sheltering behind that rock in the storm.

On 6 January 1879 he crossed the Ncome River (site of the earlier pivotal battle of Blood River between the Boers and Zulu army in the time of King Dingane) and caught up with the British army just inside Zululand: endless wagons, teams of oxen, whips cracking, drivers yelling, horsemen galloping to and fro, general bedlam.

The procedure for joining went something like this:

Officer to lad:

"That your horse?"

"Yes, sir."

"That your saddle and bridle?"

"Yes, sir."

"Can you shoot?"

"Yes, sir."

"Where did you learn?"

"In the Transvaal, sir, with the Boers, shooting game."

"How old are you?"

"Seventeen, sir." (What was one year's difference?)

"See him equipped, sergeant, and put him in a good tent."

One seasoned soldier tried with some persistence to warn him to turn around and head back to from wherever he had come. The officer in charge of the Frontier Light Horse was Major Redvers Buller, later the general who led the British army at the beginning of the Anglo-Boer War when it got its imperial nose bloodied by General Louis Botha's Boers on the Natal Front.

When a corporal showed Mossop to his tent he was greeted by banter directed towards him that he found course and offensive to his ears but that today you would hear in any high school team's changing room, and even then it would be on the tame side:

"Where did you find it Corporal?"

"Gentlemen, I am proud to say my wife presented me with him just three weeks ago today. You are to nurse, feed, and look after it; them's orders."

"Hi, Corporal, you've forgotten the feeding bottle."

"I will send one."

"Hi, Corporal, fill it with rum. The poor little mite will get the tummy ache and we can dose it."

Another: "Hi, Corporal, you have forgotten the bib."

"Go to hell."

Over the following months, by and by, Mossop was involved directly or indirectly in several conflicts which at the time were all significant, but have now been all but forgotten. One such incident occurred on 12 March with a company of the 80th Regiment under Captain Moriarty. They were escorting a wagon train across the Ntombi River where they were ambushed by a Zulu regiment and forty-four British soldiers were killed. The FLH gave chase across the river but did not manage to make contact with the retreating Zulu force.

Life on the march was hard for the FLH. They were permanently on patrol, had no tents or equipment other than one blanket each and were soaked to the skin, cold and hungry almost all the time. They slept packed tightly together for warmth while rain beat down upon them. Although, the young soldier observed, what little they had was a lot more than their Zulu foe.

However, if they were lying in the rain and mud, so was Major Buller. He endured all their hardships and became something of an idol to the fighting men under his command. It certainly toughened up young Mossop, made a man of him you might say, and it was the basic training he needed for the task that lay ahead.

A campaign was planned to punish Chief Umbelene in revenge for the losses inflicted on Captain Moriarty's men. Joining the four hundred men of the FLH commanded by Major Buller was Weatherly's Horse plus around forty Boers from Peter Uys Raff's Corps. On 28 March they rode out of their base at Kambula and made camp that evening at the base of Hlobane Mountain.

The plan was to storm the mountain by darkness and surprise Umbelene's men on the summit that was protected on three sides by steep cliffs and accessible by only a narrow neck on its eastern flank. The British force made fires as if settling down for the night. When darkness settled on the land they began to climb the mountain, leading their horses up the steep slope.

It was a pitch dark night and you can imagine the confusion as the unit stumbled over boulders, bushes, each other and themselves, horses and men all making a big commotion. To top that, thunder clouds began to gather over the mountain and lightning flashed in the night. This would have caused greater confusion for the advancing force and would have made them all the more visible to the highly organised and alert defenders.

"Oh, that climb!" lamented Mossop. "We were floundering and falling in the darkness, the horses plunging and slipping behind; those in front suddenly bounding forward over a boulder or as suddenly backing, crushing us against the horse behind."

Then came sheets of rain, beating them back, lightning and stinging rain blinding the struggling men and horses and drenching them, but they dared not halt and be caught out on the steep slopes when daylight broke. Still some men were picked off by Zulu sentries. The storm abated just as one party reached the summit, the stars came out – but not long thereafter the sky in the east began to pale.

Mossop was in the rear guard of four sections, and as they reached the summit a Zulu impi closed in around them. The Zulus advanced slowly, cautiously, moving from boulder to boulder. Once within range, they began to snipe at the British soldiers caught out on relatively open ground, firing the Martini-Henry rifles they had looted at Isandhlwana. Very soon the sunshine turned from warming and drying to hot and stifling. All too soon there was precious little water left in their canteens.

The Zulus were gathering in large numbers and the rear guard was soon in trouble and cut off from their approach route. The only possible escape was down a narrow defile in the western cliffs, but they could hear heavy fire coming from that direction. That was when they realised the main detachment of the Zulu force was closing in from behind them.

An officer, face blackened, galloped up to Mossop's unit and shouted that they were to hold their position at all costs and then charged off again. They well knew what that meant. Just then the fearsome battle cry "*Usutu*" rang out and the Zulu unit charged.

The hill top was crowded with running, leaping, bounding black soldiers, their war shields flashing black and white in the sun. This was the pride of King Cheteswayo's army, some twenty-five thousand battle-hardened warriors, half of whom were closing in with their famous pincer, or horns of the buffalo, formation. The other half of the force had surrounded the base of the mountain to cut off any retreat or escape.

Soon the Zulus were among the Redcoats and colonials, deftly wielding their dreaded stabbing spears, the *iklwa* (*ik!* as it went in, *lwa!* as it came out). Then a group of Zulus in front and to the one side charged en masse.

"We did not need any orders; we knew what we had to do. As one man we rose like a covey of partridges and ran for the horses" (which had been tethered about fifty metres to their rear).

The Zulu soldiers preferred close combat and were busy with their stabbing spears. They rushed past Mossop as he reached his horse, seemingly more intent on reaching those of his comrades with beards. One Zulu warrior did stab him in his left arm, but with his right he managed to swing his carbine round and fire off one killing shot through the man's shield.

Then he was on Warrior, a dark bay with black points which he'd bought from an African in the Transvaal, and they were bolting for the gap to the west. Mossop passed Weatherly's Horse going in the opposite direction and they exchanged a few observations.

"You are going in the direction of the main Zulu force," Mossop informed the major, who had his young son with him.

"There's Zulus everywhere, son," the officer replied, obviously searching for another way down the cliffs.

Our young protagonist rode into a hollow, in which were hiding several hundred Zulus ready to ambush anyone who sought to escape that way. Immediately they began shouting and formed a half-moon around him, thereby cutting off any attempt of a dash to the south or east. To the north were the worst of the cliffs, to the east Weatherly's doomed outfit. Warrior realised the predicament and was dancing under his rider.

The Zulu formation started closing in so Mossop gave his horse its head. Warrior bolted straight ahead, making for the centre of the crescent. Mossop tried to rein him in but to no avail. Warrior zigged and the impi directly ahead followed his movement. Then he zagged and others tried to follow his movement. This opened up a small gap through which horse and rider shot.

Two Zulus tried to close the gap and Warrior leaped right at them, causing them to crouch and protect themselves with their shields. "When he was dashing into the line of Zulus I thought that the horse had gone mad, but it was not so; every sense he had was on high alert."

Mossop remembered seeing a bushbuck behave in the same way when set upon by hunters with spears. It would jump directly at the man guarding the spot it had selected as its escape route.

"It was fortunate I had learned to sit tight in the saddle, and especially when the horse swerved for the gap, as was done so unexpectedly; had I not gained experience in the Transvaal with the horse swerving from the wildebeest rolling-spots, and been chastised by the little Bushman Geswent, for falling, I might have been unseated."

The fleeing man noticed a group of riderless horses bunched up along the distant cliff edge, so he made for the spot. There he found other members of his unit peering over the edge. His blood went cold, he recalls, although that was as likely from bleeding as from what confronted him: a near vertical pass jammed with men and horses, all stumbling and falling, while Zulus picked them off from the flanks.

"Many glancing sights I had seen that day of the Zulus with some of our men, who had fallen into their hands – dead or alive, I do not know! It is not good to write about such things."

The man at Mossop's side had seen enough. He put the muzzle of his carbine in his mouth and blew his brains out. Mossop let out a yell, let go of his horse's reins and took a leap of faith. He lurched, rolled, stumbled, sometimes over dead horses, or boulders, or dead Zulus, or his own.

"Suddenly a grip of steel was on my shoulder and I received such a clout on my ear that had the grip not been there to hold me up I would have shot yards away.

"'Where is your horse?' someone shouted.

"I looked into the face of Major Buller.

"'Up there', I said and pointed up the pass.

"'Go back and get him. Don't leave him again,' he shouted."

Mossop climbed back up the pass and located his horse, who met him with a loud whinny. Horses all around them were being set upon by Zulus with their long-bladed spears, but the maw of the pass was now completely cut. So Mossop took himself and Warrior down the only other break in the cliffs he could find. They both simply leapt over the edge, but it was way too steep to keep their footing and both fell and tumbled, hitting rocks and bouncing off them, sparks flying where the horse's iron shoes hit rock.

They continued to fall, unable to gain any footing, going over ledge after ledge. They were separated when a horse, already stabbed to death, came flying through the air and landed directly on top of Mossop. He was saved by falling between two boulders with the horse on top.

It knocked him flat, winded and jammed in a tight spot. He managed to squeeze and wiggle and shove his way out from under the dead horse and then crawled, rolled and stumbled on down. On a very narrow bit of level ground he found Warrior waiting for him, no limbs broken.

However, the saddle had been damaged and some of the iron bars were sticking into Warrior's sides. Mossop took off his jacket and placed it under the saddle for extra padding. The man's hat and rifle remained under the dead horse. Still, he had the sense to see that he needed to knot his mount's reins to prevent them tripping up the horse, which was amazing they had not yet done so.

They made their separate ways down the rest of the steepest part of the mountain, having taken a course none of the enemy had thought was worth blocking. On the talus slope that formed a steep apron around the hill, Mossop found his horse waiting for him. Both had wounds and were blood soaked, but they were alive. Mossop did, however, note that Warrior's head hung uncharacteristically low.

Below them the second half of Cheteswayo's army was swarming. There was much gunfire but Mossop saw a ridge that offered a small chance of escape, if only he and Warrior could hold out. They were both more seriously injured than the man realised, had suffered loss of blood and neither had eaten or had any water since the previous day. As soon as the rider mounted he realised his mount was in distress.

They were walking along and Mossop had nodded off in the saddle when he was alerted by Warrior who had broken into quick, short steps – a sure sign that trouble was coming. He opened his eyes to be confronted by a group of Zulus approaching at a silent run, their spears already raised to strike. In his normal state the horse would have sensed the oncoming danger, which further showed he was in bad shape.

Horse and rider made it through and bounded over the next rise where they found a group of ragged, bloodied British soldiers surrounding and tending to one of their wounded on the ground. In charge was the familiar face of Major Buller. Mossop admits to nearly bursting into tears.

"A little to the north of this group was a big German, standing on a rock, his clubbed rifle crashing down upon the heads of a number of Zulus surrounding him. I could hear his gruff voice shouting something like 'Hooroo, hooroo!' He bent gradually under the spears and fell."

Groups of Zulus were closing in, picking off the British soldiers as they found them. Buller ordered Mossop to take off immediately down the slope in the only direction that offered a chance of escape. All around him the teenager saw British soldiers in ones, twos and threes all making for the safety few would find. When he came to a small, muddied trickle of water he knew he had to dismount and he and Warrior drink or die from thirst, if not Zulu spears.

This revived them just in time to flee the next wave of Zulus sweeping down the hillside, but Warrior's head was still hanging low, indicating possible internal injuries, and Mossop's legs would not cooperate. He shouted at them, hit them with his fists, tried to pull himself up with the stirrups, looked up and saw a wall of advancing black men almost at the stream. Without remembering how, he found himself in the saddle and they made off, but he could not get his feet into the stirrups and had to clench with his thighs, while Warrior could manage only a trot.

To make matters even worse for the horse, Mossop's jacket had worked out from under the saddle and the metal bars again pierced the horse's sides. Mossop had no time to try to fix it. Escape was their immediate and most urgent priority.

Once they had put some distance between themselves and their pursuers, Mossop did consider stopping to make adjustments to the saddle, but he was worried that should he dismount he would not be able to get back up into the saddle. Onwards they went and Warrior seemed to pick up the pace.

Through the afternoon Warrior was able to outrun several more attempts to cut them off. At times they outpaced or outflanked large contingents of Umbelene's men, an evidently endless host marching steadily onwards. At times groups were sent to try to cut them off, but each time the horse found a way through. Eventually that evening they reached the safety of Kambula.

"Many men in South Africa have been killed in such scraps as the one on the Hlobane Mountain, and if they could but relate their experiences before going under, this account of my escape would be very tame reading," he insists.

Mossop tended Warrior, did as best he could for his wounds, gave him water and food but the pony only made a feeble attempt to nibble. The well bloodied young man went off to tend to himself. He fell asleep almost immediately but awoke feeling much better than he might have guessed. He was the only one from the mess tent who returned from the battle.

He found Warrior laying on the ground as if dead. He was still alive but only just. Mossop knelt down and lifted his pony's head onto his lap. The horse gave one pitiful whinny, shuddered twice and then lay still.

"Only a little Basuto pony, but he had a great heart, and – he loved me."

That is only a quarter way into Mossop's autobiography. Mossop went on to many other adventures, finding his way to Mozambique where he farmed with some success. He married and had two sons.

While I was editor at *Getaway* magazine a man pitched up to show me a book he had published. He introduced himself as Gordon Button, a grandson of Mossop, and asked if I would care to review it. Since he'd driven all the way from Plettenberg Bay I felt obliged to accept.

The book had been compiled from the notes his grandfather had left and which he'd deemed worth saving, publishing and sharing. I have before and since seen many less-than-riveting home-published books of parents' and grandparents' memoirs.

However, I am also always willing to give a book a chance. I opened this one, entitled *Running the Gauntlet*, and was gripped from page one. It now sits on one of my bookshelves shoulder-to-shoulder with the likes of *Jock of the Bushveld*, *Memoirs of a Game Ranger* and *Commando*.

One thing that, for me, elevated this tale above so many others like it was the humility of the writer and the fact that he completely lacked the pervading colonial bigotry of the time. He was in many ways a simple man, but in his heart, his mind and his soul George Joseph Mossop was clearly a noble one.

In conclusion he notes that many people (then as now) are fond of reflecting about the good old days, but that for his part, he'd be damned if he could know where the good days came or went. "Hard old days would be nearer the mark."

Helen Martins – A Glow in the Dark

How the witch of Nieu Bethesda brought light to the Great Karoo

WE SET OFF FROM GRAHAMSTOWN one Friday afternoon in the late 1970s in a borrowed Ford Escort and managed to fill up in Cradock. Those were the days of fuel rationing so you had to plan a road trip carefully. A friend of mine at Rhodes University had asked if I would be driver and navigator for "a mission" that weekend. I had done a bit of exploring around the country but had not as yet penetrated very far into the Great Karoo.

She'd decided to do her masters degree in fine art on the life and work of someone who lived in a place called Nieu Bethesda, which sounded apprehensively Old Testament to me, an idealistic journalism student. My accomplice had vague directions and a contact name. She described in the briefest terms a farming community where a woman named Helen Martins had created some kind of sculpture garden that you entered through a moon gate into an apparently enchanting place full of fantastical sculptures.

My friend had been inspired at a talk by South African primitive art guru Walter Batiss but she was short on details. With the typical prejudices of youth, I imagined the neatly attired wife of a prosperous sheep farmer who had turned their *werf* into a kind of Boere Baroque extravaganza (or "extra gavanza" as I once heard), all neatly tended by tenant labourers.

As the sun set in our eyes we climbed the Stormberg range, breached the Bamboesberg, crossed the Plains of Camdeboo (or Bruintjieshoogte as it was known in former times), and began our ascent of the Stormberg in the dark.

We navigated winding Rubidge Kloof through the tunnel vision of our meandering headlight beam: a spotted eagle-owl sitting on a fence post, a bat-eared fox scurrying across the road, a mongoose darting by. We entered a valley, the nature or dimensions of which I could not discern in the darkness.

I knew very little about the mission, but my travelling motto in those days was borrowed from the Romans – *veni, vedi, vici*: you went, you saw, you dealt with it. For example, I did not know that we'd be staying in a village and not on a farm, or that the subject of our investigations was dead. She had died a few years previously and we would be the guests of a Mevrou Claasens.

Around eight o'clock we knocked on her door and she welcomed us warmly. I think it was fellow student Carl who noted that Afrikaners had big hearts – if they liked you. Double that for Karoo *volk*. Mevrou had been the village postmistress and self-appointed mayor for many years but now wanted to retire to be nearer her children and grandchildren.

The village school (whites only) had closed some time previously, the dominee no longer visited once a month from Graaff-Reinet to conduct Sunday services. Even the postal service had given up on the place. Those were days long before the village had any guesthouses, restaurants or art galleries. There was just a general store with the usual paraffin, Lifebuoy soap, canned pilchards, twice-a-week delivery of fresh bread and milk from Graaff-Reinet or Middelburg and a diesel bowser tank outside.

But Mevrou had a conundrum: she felt she could not abandon

Miss Helen's (as she called the older, deceased woman) legacy to the elements, or worse. She fed us hearty soup and homemade bread and by and by she opened up to the two wide-eyed innocents seated in her doily draped lounge.

Helen Elizabeth Martins was born in the village in 1897, the youngest of six children, and trained as a teacher at the college in Graaff-Reinet. She had married a fellow teacher, Willem Pienaar (a "charming philanderer") and they'd moved upcountry. He joined the diplomatic corps and they lived for several years in New Orleans, but clearly things did not work out well and they divorced in 1926. She returned to the village to live with and care for her aging parents.

Our host was not as closed-minded as some of her neighbours who, she intimated, peered at one other through their keyholes with both eyes at the same time, but still one had to be circumspect about these things. There were things that needed to be explained in order for us to understand whatever it was that awaited us in the morning.

Mevrou confessed that she was the somewhat reluctant custodian of whatever it was that Miss Helen had bequeathed the village. She was eager that we give her an opinion of the place because no one else in or around the village seemed much interested in the crazy old lady and her even crazier "art".

We did learn that the famous son of the Karoo and man of letters Athol Fugard owned a cottage in the village and that he was one of only a very few people who had befriended the woman during her creative period. (He wrote the powerfully evocative play *The Road to Mecca* about her.)

There was also the local Telkom technician who would pop in to see Miss Helen. She would get him to draw the things she wanted to make, like the owl-camel in the yard. The local dominee, on the other hand, who tried hard to make her admit to the errors of her pagan ways, was not a favourite.

We learned about an affair with a local builder, a married man, and rumours of a pregnancy and even an abortion. Already a recluse, Miss Helen was pretty much ostracised by the pious farming community. For them she made a special two-faced owl in her garden of other-worldly delights.

After her long-ill mother Hester, whom she adored, died in 1941 she was left to care for her father Petrus Jakobus Martins, whom she did not adore. Here Mevrou Claasens couched her words in protective sheep's clothing but we got the gist that it was not a happy time. In fact, on some dimly suggestive level, it was an abusive relationship.

We got the picture that he was a heavy drinker and a religious hypocrite. Helen retreated deeper into the dark recesses of her home. Her best friends were the birds she kept: owls and doves. Helen draped chicken wire on poles to cover the garden and keep them in but village children would throw rocks onto the netting and break it. They would also throw stones onto the roof of the house of "the witch". When her father died in 1945 she commenced work on the house.

I went to sleep on a camping mattress in the lounge that night and was surprised by the crisp morning air. The village was cradled in a high, green valley, tall poplar trees lining the gravel streets, sheep grazing in lucerne fields and furrows carrying fresh mountain water down from the high ground.

All the streets seemed to converge on a great pyramid of rock that I learned was called the Compasberg. The valley was no Shangri La, but it had a refreshing mountain countenance and verdant setting like nothing I had expected to find in the middle of the arid Karoo.

The locals called that great geological projection the Matterhorn of the Karoo. Years later when I climbed its snow-covered summit in winter I could see why. Nieu Bethesda seemed like a land of milk and honey, but I remembered the old saying that in places like this you had to bring your own cows and bees.

From a distance the Owl House looked like just another typical Karoo dorp "huisie" of Victorian vintage. There was a central front door, sliding sash window on either side and steps leading up from the dusty street to a narrow stoep that was shaded by a curved corrugated-iron roof awning.

On the stoep floor were some small cement statues of owls with big coloured glass eyes and lots of bird droppings. The panes of one sash window had two faces staring at us, bright yellow sun faces. Mevrou Claasens had given us a key to the front door but in Miss

Helen's days she made you enter through her Moon Gate. Since her death it had been barred with chicken wire.

The place inside was immediately musty and dusty and cluttered and dishevelled, left as it was the day Miss Helen was taken away by ambulance. It was far more Karoo Narnia than Boere Baroque.

We had been forewarned and were to confirm that the owner did not care much for worldly things. Everything was vividly coloured. Every ceiling of the narrow house, every cornice, every wall, every door jamb, every window frame, window sill and window pane was covered with brightly coloured crushed glass. The walls and ceilings in neat geometric patterns.

Table tops, chairs, trunks, even an old leather suitcase were covered in glass fragments that had been glued carefully into place. And mirrors. Every room had mirrors, some just one or two but other rooms several. Mevrou Claasens told us there had been more but that after her death some of Miss Helen's relatives had come and taken the ones they fancied.

Any money anyone gave her for clothes or food would be spent on mirrors. She designed them herself and had a glassmaker in Port Elizabeth make them up.

We found a framed photo of Helen obviously taken in her later years. She wore a faded house frock, was rake thin, bent over and – if you looked carefully – her hands were claw-like. Apparently she was very sensitive about her arthritic hands and would try to hide them whenever anyone came around. Also her feet, which had been mutilated by a botched operation to fix bunions. She was greatly embarrassed when she learned she had once refused entry to the famous Walter Battis.

The floor of the house was cluttered with what to me looked very much like junk, including suitcases, boxes and plastic shopping bags. There was a strange creature lying in the main passageway. I cannot recall what the head looked like but the body was made from a springbok skin out of which stuck two legs, one with a foot and the other a hoof. It was all unexpected and quite unnerving.

The kitchen and pantry were even more disordered. There was food everywhere. Not fresh or even tinned, but in typical Karoo style: preserved food in glass jars, sealed and never opened. The table, counter tops and pantry shelves were groaning with preserves. Looking out to the garden you could see the diffused silhouettes of various forms.

If the interior was exotic, what beckoned out the back was a positive Oriental bazaar of creativity. Weeds and grass had grown head height and there was broken glass and a few broken or crumbled sculptures, but most were mercifully intact, and there were lots of them. You could barely move without bumping into owls or camels or peacocks or mermaids perched on glass-bottle turrets proffering drinks, or glass-bottle gazebos and many other fantastical things.

They were all decorated with coloured glass. Some just the eyes but others the entire form, all dazzling and sparkling in the early morning sunlight. After we had got our bearings on the place – and it was not a large area – we could make out the central piece of yard was a caravanserai with camels and turbaned "wise men" all facing the east, some of them pointing to stars fixed atop metal poles.

It was all quite bewildering, and it was only much later that day that we discovered the prose, words and sentences snipped out of sheet metal and affixed to the perimeter fence with bloudraad. Bit by bit I started to decipher the words, then the sentences. I felt like an archaeologist solving a puzzle in the desert: "The moving finger writes, and having writ moves on … nor all thy tears wash out a word of it …" Bits were missing and some were falling or had fallen off, but I knew it well enough to recognise the *Rubáiyát of Omar Khayyám* (the FitzGerald translation, naturally).

You couldn't grasp it all in just one day. Not just the fabric of the place, but the meaning of it all. Focusing too intently on the individual pieces was like trying to count the leaves on a tree when your real intention was to navigate the forest. You needed to step back a bit in order to avoid emotional schizophrenia, induced by the sparkling kaleidoscope of stimuli. Then you got it. Of course, it was about the light! Helen Martins's life work had been to bring light into her otherwise dark world.

Mevrou Claasens told us later that Miss Helen had built her glass bottle gazebos as observatories. She would place a stool inside and watch the full moon rise, its reflected light refracting in the red glass prisms. The mirrors inside the house were also placed so she could see the rising full moon wherever she was in the house.

Rummaging around inside we found more clues: an empty tin of Sunbeam floor polish in the pantry – the sunny faces on the front window, postcards from relatives travelling abroad – some of the more fanciful statues, artful black-and-white nude poses of a young woman, a niece apparently – some of the more elegant, balletic sculptures.

Among all the statues and sculptures the piece de resistance was the owl-camel. It was much more refined and carefully rendered than the earlier, clunky and inexpertly plastered camels in the yard. It appeared that the big change in her work came in the mid-1960s when a local man, Koos Malgas, came to work for her. You can bet neither could have foreseen that the Martins-Malgas artistic collaboration would one day be acknowledged worldwide as one of the finest known examples of "outsider art".

Where the owl-camel was, artistically speaking, the high point, the emotional low point was the outside lean-to room. On the step was painted "The Lion's Den" and, in harsh contrast to the rest of the house, it was painted completely and oppressively black. This was where Helen's father had spent his last years and it was only after he died that she began to work the place over.

In a corner of the garden was a corrugated-iron awning under which stood a wooden bench. On it was fixed a rusted old coffee grinder with heaps of glass bottles lying all around. Miss Helen would pay village kids a rand or two for each coloured bottle they brought her, then grind them up for her interior decorations. Unfortunately all that glass dust got in her eyes and, over the years, brought the onset of blindness. Once everything inside the house had been covered she ventured outdoors.

We went in search of Koos Malgas and found him in the coloured township on what I guess you would call the other side of town. These ghettos are the dark alter ego of apartheid South Africa and just about every town has one white side connected to a black or brown one by an umbilicus of economic dependency.

All the people in the township were clearly of strongly Khoi ancestry. This valley would have been deep in the heart of Bruintjieshoogte, the last stronghold of Khoi resistance against white colonial expansion. The leader of the Khoi people here was Dawid Stuurman, a character we have already come across in a previous chapter of this book.

This would have been a piece of history worth knowing at the time, because many of the Khoi-coloured people living in Nieu Bethesda would have been descendants of Dawid Stuurman and his comrades. I am sure that to Koos Malgas we were just two spoilt, rich white folks.

He was extremely reticent and did not care to indulge in either small talk or big talk. I thought it might be my extremely limited command of Afrikaans at the time that was the barrier, but probably not. I did not appreciate it then, but I do now: he was not willing to give up his intellectual property rights to any strangers who happened by.

It was obviously Martins's intention to fill the entire yard, much as she had done with the house but, by and by, what with failing eyesight, arthritis and frail health, in August 1976 she took a bottle of caustic soda from the pantry and drank, intending to end her life there and then. It took three agonising days for the powerful alkali (also known as lye, or sodium hydroxide) to eat her insides away and bring final relief from the pain of this world.

On that first trip to see the Owl House and Camel Yard the place radiated a form of emotional and artistic nuclear energy that was heady and disorienting. I suspect the mix of Nieu Bethesda and Helen Martins was too powerful a potion for my sensitive artist friend and as far as I know she never returned.

I have, many times, but since the Owl House was tidied up it lost much of its charm for me. Now I visit only to show anyone who has not before seen the place, but I am mightily relieved it was saved, and in 1989 declared a provisional national monument. We have Mevrou Claasens largely to thank for keeping the place locked up until it gained wider appreciation.

As compensation I have discovered that Nieu Bethesda is the geographical, geological, palaeontological and very possibly the mystical epicentre of South Africa. The place can put a spell on you.

Jack and Sally – True Love at the Place of Beans

The curious tale of how Jack Barber found the meaning of life, then lost it

I NEVER MET JACK OR SALLY BARBER. They had died long before I discovered the Garden of Eden that is shown on maps of the Wild Coast as Mbotyi. It means "place of beans", apparently from the cargo of a ship wrecked there some time long forgotten. Mbotyi lies about midway Port St Johns and Waterfall Bluff.

I was fishing at Shark Point, not catching, mind, just fishing, when a man came up and stood off to my right. He watched for a long while, as fishers will. No judgement, no advice, no clever observations.

After a long while he said, as though to the waves: "There was a big fire made here once. Not a wild fire, a bonfire, here on this point."

I pulled in my line, got two beers out of my cooler box and offered him one. We each took a swig and gazed out to sea. It was only after his second swig that he picked up the story: "There was a ship passing. It, the fire, was made for someone aboard that ship …"

I felt like a wedding guest in a scenario where the wild-eyed ancient mariner fixes someone on the steps of the church to tell them his story.

Fear not, fear not, thou Wedding-Guest …

Alone on a wide wide sea!

My fishing pal's story began with Jack Barber shipping off to France during World War I. I remember that before the "great" war he had played soccer for Scotland, but cannot recall if he was Scottish but lived in South Africa, or came to South Africa only after the war.

At any rate he, along with several millions like him, was wounded in the terrible trenches along the Western Front. It would have been late in the war because when he was evacuated to a hospital behind the lines he was tended by, among others, volunteer American nurses, the United States having joined the merry fray only in April of 1917.

He seems to have hit it off with one nurse in particular, Sally Barnes, the scion of a well-to-do family of Boston. After the war ended in 1918 they went their respective ways, she back to Massachusetts and he to South Africa, but continued to correspond.

The next stanza of this epic tale takes place in 1922 when title deeds were granted to Johannes Victor Kottich and Jack Barber on a four hectare piece of crown land at the Mbotyi River mouth where they duly set up a trading store.

The title document stipulated that the "quit rent" payment would be £1 a year in perpetuity. Rights did not include any gold, silver or precious stones "which may from time to time be discovered on the land". A rather mysterious and romantic clause for a title deed, except that then, and even until quite recently, stories circulated about a fabulous treasure having gone down thereabouts on the British East Indiaman *Grosvenor*, wrecked back in 1782.

Over the years many people have searched for it, some sinking considerable effort and fortunes into various failed ventures. If you have ever been to Lambasi Bay nearby you will have seen the rusted old crane that was brought down from the Reef on ox-wagons in an attempt to raise the sunken ship. There is also the stonework around a tunnel entrance where some deluded soul thought he could tunnel under it: did he think he could drain the Indian Ocean, one wonders!

Back at Mbotyi details are frustratingly scanty. Did Vic Kottich live on the Wild Coast prior to 1918 as one of the hardy bunch of trading store entrepreneurs, or did he and Jack go there in order to forget the din of the world? Did Jack and Vic meet during the war, while convalescing maybe, or had they been friends beforehand? I do not know. Maybe I was rebaiting or perhaps resupplying from the cooler box and missed some details around this point.

Anyway, what was special about their piece of land was that it is one of only a very few places on the Wild Coast – otherwise all tribal land controlled by various traditional chiefs – where freehold title is conferred upon the holders. At this stage Vic begins to fade from the scene, but we learn that Jack fitted into the place like one of those Nguni cows you'll see relaxing on the beaches here.

If Jack was not happy he seems at least to have been in his element. When he was not leaning on the store's counter, made from a solid slab of yellowwood, he spent most of his days walking the coastline, always barefooted, accompanied by an eager pack of dogs. We can judge he was well satisfied with his lot for two reasons. The first is that he bought out his partner Vic. The second is that around the same time he sent a letter to Sally proposing marriage. Much to his surprise, my fellow fisher recounted, she accepted.

During the course of messages crisscrossing the wide Atlantic Ocean, how, Sally asked, would she know when she was passing the place where her new home in Africa was to be? Jack told her he would calculate when her ship was due to pass and he would make a fire big enough for her to see (ships in those days always passing within sight of land). On the appointed day in 1929 Jack built and lit his huge bonfire.

Sally set sail from New York and, together with an impressive trousseau, crossed the Atlantic to London, from there to Cape Town and then Durban (passing Mbotyi about a day's sailing from her port of disembarkation). From Durban she travelled down to Port Edward by narrow gauge steam train. Once there her boxes were loaded onto an ox-wagon and up she climbed.

A reference to women's fashions of the time states: "Traveling in the 1920s was a dirty affair. Cars were dusty and trains were hot. People were bound to be a wrinkled mess by the time they arrived at their destination. Traveling clothes were simple suits and low profile shoes. Colours were drab grey, brown and blue that showed the least amount of dirt possible. Materials that wrinkled, like linen and cotton, were avoided, and instead knit, wool or sturdy cotton blends were preferred."

In those days access from the main road past Lusikisiki down through the forested slopes to the coast at Mbotyi could be hazardous, especially during summer when heavy rains turned the slippery clay surface to goo. At all times of year there were dangerous creatures afoot in the forest.

Right up until the mid-1930s when a half-decent road was built, people would park their cars at the top of the escarpment and walk the final eight kilometres to the beach. These would have been mainly Jack's fishing friends for whom he built a number of simple cottages close to the trading store, which by then had become known as Barber's Camp. If word got to him that a party had got mired, he would send up porters to help carry supplies and sometimes a wagon to pull out a stricken vehicle.

I don't know what time of year Sally arrived, but something that stands out in the story is that she never opened her trousseau, and also once there never again left. It seems she was enchanted not only with Jack but also with the place. She led an active life, horse riding each day while Jack went about on his walks and tending to the community and becoming its nurse, fairy godmother and guardian angel.

The couple had no children, seeming to be more than contented, she administering to the bodies and souls of the community, riding village to village to help clear up infections and disputes, while Jack saw to their more worldly needs. They were quite happy with their own company, living in harmony with the local people and the abundant natural environment of the Mpondoland coast. The leafy path from where the trading store used to stand, and now a hotel, down to the beach is still known as Sally's Alley.

However, the fairytale was always going to have to end, in their case earlier than nature might have allowed. Sally got sick and, by and by, died sometime in the late 1950s. By all accounts Jack was heartbroken; he hit the Scotch hard and deteriorated rapidly. Jack died in a fire that consumed his cottage, himself and his dogs. Some insisted it was suicide, others argued he never would have deliberately burned his dogs.

While the story of Jack and Sally ended there, the spellbinding saga of Mbotyi continued. Not only had Vic and Jack found a celebrated beauty spot, their precious title deeds were coveted up and down the coast. Vic meanwhile had retired to a fishing shack near the store where apparently he chose morphine as his companion and also did not make an old corpse.

By 1960 the only buildings left standing on the site were the old corrugated-iron trading store with its yellowwood counter, a cottage and the few shacks that had been built to shelter intrepid holidaymakers. The Barber estate was auctioned off to three traders from Mount Frere who did nothing much there other than go fishing. A few more (illegal) holiday shacks materialised over the next two decades.

However, one man was left smarting. Among the bidders on the day was one Khotso Sethunsa, a traditional doctor who was reputed to be the most powerful sangoma in the region. He'd made a small fortune dispensing muti and had built mini palaces in Kokstad, Matatiele and Lusikisiki. The latter can be seen in the main road of the town, a high unkempt wall surmounted by eagles and rampant lions.

The ostentatiously dressed and genial man was rumoured to have a large fortune. He claimed to have been the grandchild of President Paul Kruger's coachman and knew where the legendary gold bullion from the Zuid-Afrikaansche Republiek lay buried. To keep up the ruse he would celebrate each Kruger's Day with much fanfare. It is much more likely that if he had stumbled on any loot it would have been one of the bags of precious stones known to have been lost or discarded by the straggling survivors of the *Grosvenor*.

On auction day at Mbotyi it was assumed a forgone conclusion that "Doctor Khotso" would snap up the land which everyone knew he had eyed for a long time, but that particular day seems to have found him cash-poor and the deeds were knocked down for a mere

£50 to the three white businessmen. Khotso was bitter and swore a curse on the place.

His first encounter with the powers of the beyond is said to have occurred when he was a kwedin, a young uncircumcised cattle herd, on the farm of a Mr Eric Scott in the Kokstad region. For some infraction the lad was beaten by his employee, on whom he then threatened revenge. This was otherwise unheard of in that feudal time and place. Soon thereafter a tornado ripped through the area and carried off most of Scott's possessions.

By the early 1980s the Mbotyi Hotel had been mothballed and two of the three partners died. In 1985 the property was sold to a Dr Mazwai from Lusikisiki. He built a modern facility (for the Wild Coast) with holiday bungalows and also upgraded the road. So things remained, largely out of sight and out of mind, until the year 2000 when two energetic businessmen from Johannesburg bought the place and turned it into one of the Wild Coast's most comely holiday spots.

Over the years the place has been the scene of a number of strange occurrences. One was the disappearance in 1967 of the two Gray children, offspring of missionaries at Mount Frere who were holidaying there. They seemed to just disappear. It was hardly surprising that all manner of ghost stories were repeated, and most of them never failed to include the legacy of Khotso Sethunsa.

Another was when rogue policeman and bank robber Andre Stander holed up in one of the fishing cottages together with his accomplice in crime Patrick McCall. They were outed by a travelling salesman who happened to pop in to Mbotyi for a bit of fishing and recognised Stander.

The salesman never split on his old drinking buddy – Stander had played MC at the man's wedding – but the rogue cop decided fleeing was the safest option. He was finally apprehended in Fort Lauderdale, Florida, when he was flagged down for a minor traffic offence. He decided once again that flight was his best option and was gunned down by the cops, the honourable way for a gangster to go.

I only wish I had paid more attention to the storyteller than to my line on that balmy day at Shark Point. I think he said his name was Peter and that he'd fallen in love with the place the first time he saw it.

He got up, dusted the back of his trousers and as a final observation said: "Over the years many people have fallen in love with Mbotyi, but none more so than Jack or Sally."

Mbotyi remains a most enchanting holiday spot, but its history is extensive and diverse. It's a head-in-the-clouds, starry-eyed kind of place, far from the madding crowds. The kind of place you could easily fall in love with, or where you could simply fall in love.

James Kitching – Bone Man of the Karoo

The man from a village who moved continents

THERE WAS AN OLD geological joke much favoured by students at the University of the Witwatersrand in the 1970s:

Knock-knock …

Who's there?

Alice

Alice who?

Alice gone

Alice gone who?

Alice Gondwanaland

An interest in all things Gondwana (as it is more correctly known) blossomed here after South Africa hosted the Second Gondwana Symposium in 1970. South Africa was once part of Gondwana, not a political affiliation but the last supercontinent known to have existed.

Supercontinents are nothing new, the oldest ones are believed to date from around three billion years ago and have been named Ur,

Arctica and Atlantica. Since then the various continental plates have formed, broken apart and reformed several times.

If you could see a time-lapse movie of the history of our planet from its earliest fiery days, the movements of the various crustal plates would resemble one of those old lava lamps that stoned undergraduates in the 1970s liked to watch as the day-glow coloured oil inside formed, floated, rose, tumbled, fused, ruptured and repeated ever so slowly.

The most recent of the supercontinents was Gondwana which consisted of most of the current southern landmasses – Africa, South America, Australia and Antarctica – as well as the Indian subcontinent (the Himalayas are a consequence of its continuing journey). Gondwana began to fracture and tear apart around a hundred and ninety million years ago (mya) – little more than a geological burp ago.

Its breakup caused one of the most impressive volcanic displays of all time: the molten lava that reached the surface formed the soft Drakensberg basalt layer, which at one time covered most of southern Africa. Lava that was trapped between rock layers underground formed iron-hard dolerite that is revealed by erosion as our flat-topped Karoo koppies.

The Gondwana conference in South Africa was big news for the earth sciences because the grand idea at the time was continental drift. The theory had been around for some time and geologists were pretty sure they could stitch together rock layers from various places around the world that at some time in the past had been Siamese twins, but there was, as yet, no absolute scientific proof.

One sure way to prove it would be if you could find the fossils of creatures that were known to have lived when Gondwana was one on any of the constituent continents of today. The Great Karoo was thought to hold much, if not most, of the evidence.

The Karoo is a multi-dimensional marvel. On the surface, in the first two dimensions, are those dream landscapes of arid plains, koppies with their flat-topped crests, with farms and villages tucked away along furtive water courses.

Among them are the characters: generous sheep farmers, sheep herders and shearers with hands and faces as dry and cracked as the mud of ephemeral pans in the dry season. Then there are the karretjiesmense, the descendants of Khoisan nomads who have never had homes as we know them, the open roads of the interior being their desiccated oyster.

Geologists know the area as the Karoo Basin because that is what it was when Gondwana existed: a huge repository of eroded silt and mud lying between great mountain ranges to the north and south. Over a period of about fifty million years the basin gradually filled up. The first, oldest and now outermost ring of the concentric Karoo sequence of rocks is the Dwyka Group.

It consists of fine dust-like particles that remain from a vast continental glacier that spanned the region when the Karoo lay over our planet's southern polar region. Today Dwyka rocks can be recognised as upward-facing, protruding "Bushman gravestones" along the N1 near Touwsrivier and the R62 between Barrydale and Ladismith.

The successive rock groups are each named after the place where they are most typical (Dwyka after the Dwyka River). Next comes the Ecca Group named after the Ecca Pass near Grahamstown. All the coal in southern Africa lies within Ecca shales. Then comes the biggest of them, the Beaufort Group that today covers about half of South Africa's land surface. Finally there is the Stormberg Group consisting of Molteno (red bed sandstone) and Clarens (cave sandstone), capped by Drakensberg basalts.

If you were to drive across the country from southwest to northeast you would be travelling through geological time. Each consecutive layer of rock you passed would be successively younger and form a new chapter in a book entitled *The Story of Life on Earth*: Table Mountain Sandstone, Bokkeveld Shale, Witteberg Sandstone (maybe a stretch of Malmesbury Shale and Old Cape Granite), then Dwyka, Ecca, Beaufort, Stormberg, Drakensberg.

Due to the very long period of sedimentation, and because the resulting horizontally stratified landscape has been little disturbed by subsequent geological events, the Karoo Basin encapsulates the longest unbroken geological and palaeontological portion of that great book. Those rock layers (I like to think of them as a multi-layered cake) are the third dimension of this story, and it is all very well for mineralogists to chip and weigh and fit them into hardness indices, but there is an even deeper story here, one that plunges us into the next dimension.

The fourth aspect is revealed by what we find trapped inside the vast rock matrix, like fruit inside a Christmas cake as big as South Africa – fossils of course. The Karoo rocks contain an unbroken record of how life on Earth evolved from extremely primitive amphibious creatures during the Dwyka-Ecca period, to the appearance of the earliest mammals, or at least very mammal-like beasts of the Stormberg period around 150 mya. From that day to this South Africa has acquired only scanty fossil-bearing geological formations.

The Gondwana Symposium discussed how all this information might bear upon proving the theory of continental drift. The fossil history of the Karoo was well documented from various collections. What they needed to find were the same creatures, fused in old stone, from other now-separated bits of Gondwana. The hunt was on.

Several months after the symposium a man named James Kitching, working in the Bernard Price palaeontology institute at Wits University in Johannesburg, got a phone call from near the South Pole. On the other end of the line was EH "Ned" Colbert, head of the US Antarctic Research Program, who had attended the South Africa think-tank. Try as they might, the Americans just could not find any fossils in the rocks of the southern continent where, they had surmised, they were most likely to be found. Kitching had been a key-note speaker at the symposium and his reputation preceded him. Come and help us, Colbert urged …

James William Kitching was born almost smack in the middle of the Great Karoo, in the tiny village of Nieu Bethesda. The family was extremely poor; what with a wife and eight children all living off the salary of father CJM "Coonie" Kitching, who was a supervisor of road repairs. He'd started working on road gangs from a very young age and by the age of sixteen was already finding fossils.

Coonie had only a rudimentary education but he knew his cambers from his culverts. What he knew ever better, and loved a whole lot more, were the fossils he frequently found in the cuttings they made in the dry, exposed slopes around them. Coonie just happened to live and work in one of the world's richest known fossil repositories, the Karoo Basin. He also had a patron who compensated him for any specimens he collected.

That man's name was Robert Broom, a Scottish medical doctor who had arrived in South Africa around the turn of the nineteenth century and become Professor of Zoology at Stellenbosch University. At the time the place was known as Victoria College and was the nursery for pastors in the ultra-conservative Dutch Reformed Church. Broom was kicked out, hardly surprisingly, for teaching the doctrine of evolution.

He set up a general practice in Pearston at the southern edge of the Great Karoo where he became an ardent amateur palaeontologist. He was hell bent on finding a connection from modern mammals back to the mammal-like (therapsid) reptiles that had been first unearthed in the Karoo earlier in the nineteenth century by men such as pioneer road builder Andrew Geddes Bain.

In the mid-1930s, at the age of 67, Robert Broom was lured away from Pearston with an offer to become a full-time palaeontologist with the Transvaal (now Ditsong) Museum. In truth, he was sinking into poverty in his Karoo backwater when then Prime Minister Jan Smuts found him the job as assistant palaeontologist in Pretoria. (A book, or at least a chapter of one, could and indeed should be written about him; if there is a father of palaeontology in South Africa, it surely is he.)

Broom himself was not so good at finding fossils and so relied heavily on others, most notably Sidney Rubidge and Coonie Kitching, to be his eyes in the field. He tried time and again to have Coonie Kitching employed at the Pretoria museum as a field collector, only to be thwarted each time by a person he refers to only as "……" (more likely what he meant was "@#$%&").

As things turned out, Pretoria's loss was the gain of merino sheep farmer Sidney Rubidge of Wellwood, whose farm lay on the approach to Nieu Bethesda. Coonie started a prodigious partnership with Rubidge and together they amassed the largest and finest private collection of Karoo fossils in existence. Of his own collection, Broom acknowledged that nearly half of it had been accumulated with the help of those two men.

Coonie Kitching's son James was the eldest of his eight children. Together with his younger brothers, Ben and Scheepers, James loved nothing more than accompanying his father on fossil-hunting expeditions disguised as work. Lessons in the village school came a dismal second. What he also learned to do was live rough, sleeping with his two brothers and their father in those old, sagging bell-shaped canvas tents one used to see along lonely roads in the Karoo whenever roads were being repaired.

It was a hard life, but clearly the Kitching family thrived on it. James discovered his first fossil at the age of six. A year later he discovered a new species which Robert Broom named *Younopsis kitchingi* (it has since been reclassified as *Hymeniacidon kitchingi*).

Later in his professional career he discovered the oldest-known dinosaur eggs. From the shape of a partially exposed skull in one of the six eggs found near Golden Gate, he correctly identified the species as *Massospondylus*, a long-necked and long-tailed fast-running lizard from the late Karoo Stormberg period.

At the conclusion of World War II James returned home from service in Italy (father Coonie also served but had died of wounds sustained in North Africa a few years earlier). In that year Robert Broom gave a talk at Wits University about the importance of collecting, preserving and studying Karoo fossils – progenitors of all mammals and, by inference, humans.

In the audience was the general manager of the Victoria Falls Power Company, Bernard Price. He was clearly impressed for he duly established an endowment of £2,000 a year to create a chair of palaeontology at the university. James Kitching was appointed as its first employee and spent his entire professional life working there.

He did not have an undergraduate degree, and yet such was his knowledge and academic standing that when he applied to read for an MSc the Wits senate consented. For his work on Permian-Triassic therapsids (Karoo mammal-like reptiles) he was awarded not the anticipated MSc but a full PhD. James Kitching remains the only South African to have gained an academic doctorate, as opposed to an honourary one, without having a standard degree. He didn't even have a matric certificate.

Kitching's fossil-hunting field trips were legendary. Someone has calculated that in his fifty-five years as a professional palaeontologist James Kitching spent more than two hundred months, nearly eighteen years, in the veld, camping and looking for fossils.

He eschewed tinned foods and knew how to keep supplies fresh for weeks without any refrigeration. His camps were always meticulously organised, like a military operation, but Kitching, the most senior man, did almost all the cooking and cleaning. "Any fool can be uncomfortable in the veld," he famously asserted. His meals were invariably prodigious and delicious, but it was as a fossil finder that his real talents shone.

James was as lean and keen as a hunting dog and could outwalk anyone else when on the trail. Each evening the fossil collectors would gather around the camp table to share their day's pickings. Most would offer meagre bone fragments, knowing well that the "master", who seemed to possess the super power of X-ray vision, would invariably pull from his haversack complete skulls, segments of skeletons, if not fully articulated ones, always trumping the others. A few days or even hours under Kitching's tutelage in the veld could turn any uncomfortable camper into a half-decent fossil detective.

When Kitching got the call from Colbert of the US Antarctic Research Program, he was there like a leopard seal chasing penguins. On his first day at the American base he requisitioned a helicopter trip in order to scout the area for likely picking fields. A particular ridge sticking out from the ice and snow caught his eye, and he asked the chopper pilot to put him down there.

On his first walk during his first day on the frozen continent, James Kitching spied the fossil remains of long-extinct creatures with which he was well acquainted from the Beaufort-era rocks around his home village. He had found the Gondwana missing link and the geological grail, conclusively proving the two land masses had been one during the Permian-Triassic period.

The remains were a specimen of *Thrinaxodon*, a genus of two-tusked proto-mammals that had lived in Gondwana around two hundred mya. It was the size of and looked something like the love child between a warthog and a leguaan (mammal-like reptiles truly). They were known as dicynodonts for the two tusk-like teeth they carried in their flat-snouted reptilian heads.

Colbert said of Kitching: "Of all the fossil hunters with whom I have been associated none is the equal of James Kitching. He has an eye for fossils that is truly phenomenal, and his ability to discover fossils in the rocks is justly celebrated on numerous continents."

It is now almost universally acknowledged that James Kitching was the most skilled and prolific fossil hunter who ever lived. When he retired in 1990 around ninety per cent of the samples in the Bernard Price Institute had been collected by or under the supervision of Kitching, or "Kitch" to his colleagues and friends. The protrusion in Antarctica on which the chopper dropped the legendary fossil hunter, which lies to the west of the Shackleton Glacier on Queen Maud Land, now bears the name Kitching Ridge.

In the early 1980s I stumbled into Wellwood Farm while on a climbing trip with my rope buddy of the time, Clive Ward. We were scouting the area prior to laying siege to the Compasberg, that needle of dolerite that stabs the Karoo sky and is often referred to as the Karoo Matterhorn, especially in winter when it is frosted with newly fallen snow.

We literally staggered in when our *iskorokoro* suffered one of its many tubercular episodes and I made one of the great discoveries of my otherwise short and miserable life. Richard Rubidge welcomed us to their guesthouse. He never charged us a cent for accommodation, for all the food they plied us with (including half a lamb that we later roasted), or for fixing our tired wagon. My guess is he took pity on us, two shaggy mountaineers.

Taking tea next to one of the giant orange trees outside the gabled homestead (Rubidges have been farming there since the mid-1800s), he told us the story of how the family got into the fossil business. It was the early 1930s and they were enjoying a picnic out in the foothills of the Stormberg mountains that encircle the farm. At some point one of the younger generation remarked to then patriarch Sidney, Richard's father, something like: "Look Daddy, this rock (in the story she had been sitting on it) looks like a monster's head."

Sidney Rubidge took a closer look and realised it really did, complete with fearsome incisors protruding from the rocky matrix. Rubidge the elder managed to get the rock onto his truck and sent it to Doctor Broom in nearby Pearston. He was already well known thereabouts as the local expert in old things.

The doctor sent a message back, thanking Rubidge and asking if he could keep the fossil of the creature that had lived there a long time ago. How long ago, the farmer wanted to know. Somewhere around two hundred million years, came the reply. Well then no, if it has been on Wellwood for so long Sidney thought it should remain there. Broom named the monster *Dinogorgon rubidgei* and the experience turned the sheep farmer into a consummate fossil collector.

Since the current fossilologist in the family, Bruce, son of Richard, was not in residence at the time of my first visit (he was busy scaling the palaeontological ladder in Bloemfontein before heading to the Bernard Price Institute at Wits), I was told I should seek out James Kitching at Wits University for more information.

Back in Joburg I duly made an appointment and expected to meet, I was not quite sure what, but probably an old curmudgeon dressed in a drab technician's coat covered in fine dust who would shuffle out musty old boxes for me to gawk at while he gawked at me. How wrong I was.

Lab coat he had, and he was certainly reticent at first, but he also had boundless energy and an astute intellect, together with a charming regional accent of the Eastern Cape. It took some time for him to warm to me. I was a news journalist at the time and he famously shunned publicity, so much so, it turned out, that when he died in 2003 he insisted no one outside his family should ever get their hands on his diaries and other papers.

Here was a man who seemed to hold the secrets of life in his hands. I have a photograph of him from that day holding in both his hands a heavy chunk of Karoo shale. On its surface is a scene carved as if in bas relief that seems to echo that most dramatic of all Hellenistic sculptures, the Laocoön, in which a man and his sons are locked in mortal battle with a sea serpent.

Except this one was for real. The scene had been whittled out of the rock using precision dental drills and revealed a contorted lattice of petrified doppelgangers of primordial creatures. The tableau revealed was the fossil of a herbivorous *Cynognathus* that had been set upon by several carnivores, possibly of the genus *Chasmatosaurus* but I'm not certain. A flash flood must have occurred, just like they still do in the Karoo, trapping those antediluvian creatures in a feeding frenzy, and there they were, trapped in time, in a solidified block of late Beaufort period mud.

Within the lowermost horizontal layers of the Karoo rock basin lie trapped the fossilised remains of the first creatures that crawled out of the Permian seas to establish beachheads on swampy land. The earliest identified is a forty centimetre, long-snouted, needle-toothed, semi-aquatic primordial lizard with webbed and clawed feet named *Mesosaurus* from the Dwyka shales, the youngest and outermost ring of the Karoo Basin.

There is a fatuous notion going around that Table Mountain has been declared one of the "new" seven natural wonders of the world (no thanks, we're good, we already have seven!), and yet there is the Karoo, our greatest natural treasure and without a shadow of a doubt one of the seven greatest palaeontological wonders of the world.

That, Alice, is the true wonder of Gondwana.[2]

2 For background information as well as some technical details in this essay I have to thank Bruce Rubidge, a son of the Karoo and current head of the Bernard Price Institute at the University of the Witwatersrand.

Nongqawuse – The Girl Who Saw Things

A teenager who convinced an entire nation to destroy its wealth and its food

MOST OF US KNOW THE STORY OF NONGQAWUSE,[3] if only vaguely. She was a teenager who saw visions in a pool. The ancestors told her the Xhosa people must kill their cattle and burn all their crops and this would prompt all their dead to rise up and help drive the British into the sea, which clearly, as history reveals, they did not.

So how could an entire people be so foolish, or duped, as to follow the word of an orphaned maiden? The full story is, as you might suspect, a lot more complicated – and catastrophic.

The area under the social microscope here is one of green hills seamed with lovely rivers coursing through wooded valleys

---

3 In Xhosa the "q" click is voiced as a "champagne cork popping" click. A learned reference describes it thus: This is a palatal click produced by pressing the front part of the tongue against the hard palate behind the front teeth and rapidly pulling it away with a "popping" sound. Give it a try.

and dark gorges, spilling over waterfalls and then spreading into shallow lagoons where they reach the coast, each flanked by golden beaches where Nguni cattle lie on the sand with looks of indolent contentment. Boys play in the surf while women with red blankets and white-painted faces collect mussels on rocks with churning tidal waters grabbing their bangled legs.

It looks like a scene of utter pastoral serenity and contentment, but closer inspection reveals that a patina of poverty and melancholy overlies the region. To understand how a place so rich in natural beauty and resources could be so socially and economically bereft we need to go back in time, back to when black pastoralists and white Trekboers first bumped up against one another in the Zuurveld, the so-called Disputed Territory of the Eastern Cape.

From the mid-1700s until the end of the eighteenth century the effective colonial frontier jumped (or was pushed) ever eastwards from the Sundays to the Fish then the Keiskamma and finally the Kei River. Skirmishes between white and black became more and more heated with cattle raids and counter raids, commando sorties and reprisal burnings of settler homesteads.

The Dutch government in Cape Town tried its best to contain these conflicts. Their policy was always to appease their black neighbours. They never really wanted a colony in southern Africa but they got one by machinations of the Trekboers, ever hungry for freedom, land and cattle. By and by, in efforts to appease all parties at the same time, agreements, treaties and arrangements were made and broken so trust was not hard currency.

Nonetheless, things were kept at a politically manageable level with the balance of power towards the numerically superior Xhosa under chiefs such as Ngqika and Ndlambe, later Hintsa (father of Sarili) and Sandile.

However, when the British grabbed the Cape Colony in the early 1800s things in the east began to change, slowly, then increasingly drastically. It seems unlikely now, although the records show it is quite true, that the colonial office in Westminster never wanted a colony in South Africa, even less so than the Dutch before them. They realised it would lead only to trouble – and very expensive trouble

– when they had much bigger fish to fry back in Europe. If it wasn't the French, it was the Austro-Hungarians, and if not them then the Russians.

All they wanted was a toehold at the Cape Peninsula in order for their navy to control the Indian Ocean. Unfortunately for them, and for the indigenous people of southeastern Africa, the people they sent out to control things on the ground along the Eastern Cape frontier were not only mostly soldiers, but The Iron Duke's men.

The Iron Duke was Wellington, hero of the Iberian Peninsula Wars and, even more significantly, Waterloo. He and his military cohorts ruled the Home Guard, seat of real power in the British Empire between 1814 and the mid-1850s. Under their influence the people who were sent out to rule the Cape were such imperial and arrogant individuals as Lord Charles Somerset, his floundering son Henry and worse.

Sir Henry Somerset accompanied his father to Africa where, it was understood, he would excel in military matters while his regal pater operated the levers of political will and force. Henry could well have been the model for Harry Flashman, the swashbuckling but inept and often foolish literary character of the Wellington era.

The fictional Flashman first appeared in *Tom Brown's School Days* and has been described as an illustrious Victorian soldier experiencing many 19th-century wars and adventures and rising to high rank in the British Army, acclaimed as a great soldier, while remaining "a scoundrel, a liar, a cheat, a thief, a coward, and – oh yes, a toady".

While Henry was certainly at least half of those, he was more Victorian Walter Mitty than scoundrel. That latter description better fits another character, also named Harry, who strutted his arrogance across the Eastern Cape veld. We'll meet him later.

As was the case of Nongqawuse, the course of Henry Somerset's life was fixed by the circumstances of his birth: he arrived at the Cape a captain in the 18th Hussars (he had served as an aide-de-camp with the rank of lieutenant during the Peninsula Wars and at Waterloo). On the Eastern Frontier he rose steadily through the ranks.

Henry was described by someone who served with him as "a pleasure-loving man of limited intelligence". When summoned to battle he was almost always too late or too early, or he would arrive at the wrong location only to return with his colours flying and reputation intact for want of getting them dirtied in the fray. Still, he seems to have been possessed of a benign nature and was well liked by comrades and foe alike. History remembers him as the senior officer too incompetent to make any enemies.

Colonel, later Lieutenant-General and then Sir, Harry Smith was an entirely different kettle of snoek. He earned his cavalier military reputation in the Peninsula Wars and later his heroic status as well as a baroncy as the hero of Aliwal in India. He was sent to South Africa by the grizzled old warriors of the Home Guard to untangle the Gordian knot of affairs on the Eastern Frontier and instill some good old military order, and instill it he did, g'dammit!

No sooner had he arrived at the Cape than a message was received on 28 December 1834, saying Xhosa forces were massing along the frontier. He enjoyed New Year's Eve in Cape Town, had three hours' sleep, got up, dressed, kissed his wife Juana farewell and with "spirits aflame" chose to ride the six hundred miles to Grahamstown instead of going by sea. Smith had met his wife Juana Maria de los Dolores de Leon on a Spanish battlefield when he was twenty-four and she just fourteen. They were married within two weeks of meeting and their passions for one another never seemed to wane.

As commander of the Eastern Frontier, Smith established King Williams Town as his headquarters. He "invited" chiefs Maqoma, Tyali, Sutu and Nqeno for the unveiling ceremony. In his first warning and insult to the chiefs he told them it was his "great place" (the name used by Xhosa paramount chiefs for their principle strongholds).

He compounded the insult by telling them he was now their inkhosi inkhulu – great chief, and they his children. He then made a show of tearing up the imaginary papers of a peace treaty that was supposed to be in force. The message was as clear as the Keiskamma River in springtime. Enmity ramped up and bellicose clouds gathered over the Amatola and Katberg mountains for what would be the Sixth Frontier War (1834–36).

The war ended when Smith lured Chief Hintsa to a peace pow-wow, only to capture and kill him instead. The chief's body was dragged behind a horse and later mutilated by Smith's troops. The colonel boasted of his feat, which shocked the white-whiskered men back in Westminster and incensed the Xhosa people. Following some other treacherous moves against the Boers in the Free State, Smith found himself transferred to India where he went on his merry swashbuckling ways.

Several changes in government in England, as well as in the colonial office, in late 1847 saw Smith transferred back to the Cape as a full major-general with military as well as political command of the Eastern Frontier. Well, you could have heard the ancestors groan.

Once again, and in fact always, in a rush Smith barely wet his lips in Cape Town before rushing on to Fort Frederick (later Port Elizabeth) where the British settlers eagerly awaited the arrival of a champion for their cause of cementing their own place in Africa.

Smith stepped, or rather was carried, ashore on 14 December 1847. According to reports published in the exceedingly partisan *Graham's Town Journal*, the colonial crowd hurrahed their hero. The paper's editor, Robert Godlonton, wrote with such inflammatory ink that he can be held as responsible as any for stirring racial rancour and enmity on the frontier.

Among the welcoming crowd he spotted his old foe Maqoma who had led the Xhosa army in 1834. Maqoma came forward and put out his hand. Instead of taking it Smith forced the Xhosa chief to prostrate himself, whereupon he placed his immaculately polished leather boot on the chief's neck, declaring: "This is to teach you that I have come to teach Kaffraria that I am chief and master here."

When Mqoma rose he retorted: "I always thought you were a great man, till this day." He intended to revenge the insult.

With only a sword in his diplomatic toolbox, every situation Harry Smith encountered was to him one that could be solved with a forward thrust. He possessed a singular ability to escalate every small skirmish to full blown war.

Had these conflicts, starting in the time of Dutch rule at the Cape in 1779, ended in 1847 with the seventh War of the Axe, they might have been relegated to the back pages of history. However, the Eighth Frontier War of 1850–53 was an entirely different kind of sardine run. It was ruthless and unforgiving, and losses on both sides were significant and brutal.

War erupted on Christmas Day 1850 and it was a bitter affair from the first assegai lunge to the last volley of lead. It involved fifteen thousand British regular troops and thousands of colonials against around ten thousand Xhosa warriors supported by an unknown number of well-armed and trained, and often mounted, Griqua-Khoi combatants.

The Battle of Boma Pass, fought in the sweltering summer of early 1851, was as bloody and unforgiving as any contested by the British Army until that date. Confusion reigned, firing at point blank range in the dark gorge, assegai to bayonet, rifle butt to knobkerrie. Men of all colours died of wounds, blood loss and terrible thirst as the battle ranged up and down the Amatola mountainside.

The Amatola mountains are to the southern or Gcaleka Xhosa what the Tsitskamma were to the Khoi, and the Witwatersrand to southern Sotho and later the Voortrekkers: a land of plenty, of sparkling streams flowing with proverbial milk and honey, undulating golden-green hills and vales. For the Xhosa it was all that and much more. It was their Valhalla, their Olympus. It was the hallowed ground of their ancestors, the spirits of the dead who guided the fortunes of the living.

The grueling conflict lasted more than two years. Not long after his humiliation at Fort Fordyce, Westminster recalled Harry Smith, deeming him too inept to rule and the man responsible for much of the aggression. He was succeeded by George Cathcart who instituted a more systematic but less violent campaign of isolating and rounding up the leaders of the "rebellion".

By February 1853 Sandile and all the other Xhosa chiefs had surrendered. This ensured the destruction of Xhosa military power and the subjugation of clans living in what is now known as the Ciskei region. Much of the most arable land was dished out to white settlers and army officers as rewards for service. Towns such as Seymour, Cathcart, even Hogsback in the very heart of the Amatolas, became white enclaves.

Then catastrophe heaped upon calamity – whatever cattle had

not been confiscated for war reparations started succumbing to a miserable sickness hitherto unknown in the region. It was lung sickness (contagious bovine pleuropneumonia), introduced from the colony. Those who had lost their lands and now their cattle were reduced to utter poverty and near starvation. It was into this scene that stepped a young Xhosa girl of no special lineage named Nongqawuse.

Nongqawuse was born in 1841 but was orphaned after witnessing her parents succumb during the "troubles" of 1850–53. She was taken into the kraal of her uncle Mhalkaza who lived close by the Gxara River, several kilometres north of the Kei and inland from where the modern seaside resorts of Trennery's and Seagulls lie. It is a lovely place, with picturesque huts and small fields, woods, streams and green grasslands tumbling to the sea. It's the kind of place you would want to raise plump cattle and succulent corn.

By 1856 the southern Xhosa were trying to start afresh, as best they could. One day in April Mhlakaza, who as the son of a councillor of Chief Sarhili was an influential man in his area, instructed his niece to go down to the river to shoo the birds that were intent on raiding his corn field there.

Xhosa people tend to live on tops of ridges and spurs, away from the water where spirits are known to lurk. You can put this down to primitive superstition, or you could surmise that it is old knowledge of the places where pythons, leopards and crocodiles liked to lurk as much as the thokoloshe.

She took with her a friend, Nombanda, and together they skipped down to the river. When they returned Nongqawuse told her uncle something astonishing, that she had met three of the ancestors who had told her a most startling thing. Nombanda insisted she had seen and heard nothing at all out of the ordinary.

Remember Nongqawuse was a teenager, just fourteen, a most impressionable age. Her uncle, a traditional healer or ugqirha, might well have influenced the girl to some extent with his knowledge of things otherworldly, not to mention the plight of their people. Was she trying to buy favour with him, as an otherwise lowly orphan, who knows?

She told her uncle the shades had spoken most clearly to her, and instructed her on exactly how their people would regain their dominion. The Xhosa people must kill all their cattle. Then, on a given day, all the dead cattle that had ever been would arise from the earth. Also, they must burn their corn fields and all the grain in their bins, and on the same day all the corn fields would arise as rows upon rows of warriors, all the dead who had ever lived, and this great army would drive the accursed mlungus into the sea.

After that the kraals would be full to bursting with fat and healthy cattle, the fields overflowing with ripe corn like grass. No crops were to be sown, but new kraals and new homes would need to be built, new milk sacks would need to be woven, new beer pots made. It would be a grand old time, but also, in order for the ancestors to bestow their blessing, the people would have to abandon witchcraft, incest and adultery.

These would have been strange instructions, especially the last set, but Mhlakaza did not seem phased. Research reveals he had spent some considerable years in the Cape (eKoloni eshonalanga – the colony of the setting sun, or west) where he had been much influenced by Christianity. It is also suggestive, Rhodes University historian Jeff Peires has surmised, that Nongqawuse was herself a victim of incest, and maybe she had early feminist sensibilities, in a strongly chauvinistic society, towards the sexual abuse suffered by the women around her. Then again maybe she was just really smart and manipulative.

Whatever her reality, her uncle seemed to accept these terms after she had described one of the ancestors who Mhlakaza recognised as his dead brother, but how would they know when the appointed day would be? Nongqawuse replied that the ancestors had told her that as well. It would be the day after the full moon in February, when a red sun would rise.

Mhlakaza sent word to Sarhili, son of Hintsa, son of Khawatu, son of the great Gcaleka from the house of Phalo, now paramount chief of all amaGcaleka. Sarhili held a big indaba to which he summoned all his councillors, his allied chiefs as well as Mhlakaza. Much beer was consumed. Many important things were debated, like the sacrificing of cattle, all their cattle; their pride, their joy, their material wealth and their corn; their staple, their bread, their staff of life.

The conclusion was that the ancestors had indeed spoken through the niece of Mhlakaza, and that this was a great thing indeed, the one for which they had been waiting and longing. Sarhili issued the order for the killing and the burning to begin.

Can you imagine the conflicted reaction? It was not surprising that the society very quickly divided into the believers and the doubters. It is perhaps not incidental that most of the believers tended to live in the lower lying areas where cattle lung sickness had inflicted the strongest blow.

The cattle killing and crop burning proceeded apace, and as it did so the madness spread among all the Xhosa people, amaGcaleka, amaRarabe, even amaThembu to the north (the amaPondo in the far north of the Transkei were too distant to be much involved). There was great anticipation when the morning after the full moon approached. The most ardent of the believers gathered on prominent places to witness the red sun rising. The day was 19 February 1857.

The predawn sky glowed salmon, a good sign. It was warm and a sea breeze bathed the coastal area. The sun peeked above a thin lamination of sea mist. It was bright orange, anticipation rose but then, instead of intensifying in colour to fiery red, it started to fade to burning yellow, then searing white as it scoured a pitiless trail across the day.

Those who had lost, thrown away, burned, slaughtered everything they had, wailed. The future looked dark indeed. Sarhili, upon whom the fate as well as the blame would eventually fall, travelled with his inner circle of councillors across the Ncezele River, the Ngogwana and the Qolora to the kraal of Mhlakaza on a knoll above the Gwara to demand an explanation.

Much beer was consumed, bones were thrown, the ancestors consulted. They told the chief that the ancestors were not satisfied; too many of the people had defied them. Too many were holding out. Sarhili returned to his Great Place, back across the Qolora, the Ngogwana and the Ncezele to near present-day Butterworth, with the message. The cattle killing and crop burning must continue with renewed vigour. There was no going back.

Eight days hence one blood red sun would rise in the east and another in the west. On the day of two suns the people must gather on a certain hill near the sea to behold the Rapture. Before the setting of the two suns there would be a great thunderstorm. Then all the dead ancestors would arise as like corn in the fields in springtime. The cattle would rise from the ground, bellowing so as to drown all sound.

The killing and burning rose to a frenzy. There was tremendous anticipation and celebration. Still there were those who did not believe and they did not kill their cattle or burn their crops, but they were the minority and many were scorned, beaten, even to death.

The women painted their faces with ceremonial white clay, the men with sacred red clay. Masses converged at the appointed place. They brought with them the very last of their food, those who had any left at all – given that the cattle killing and destroying of crops had started a full ten months earlier.

Again, as on the previous occasion, the salmon pink predawn promised a rosy outcome. You can only imagine the anticipation, the ululating as sunrise – or sunrises – approached. Everything depended on it. Then imagine the disappointment, the wailing, the crying, the sobbing, the terrible sadness and anguish of that moment when just one orange sun rose and quickly faded to bright yellow-white on the eastern horizon above the dispassionate blue of the Indian Ocean.

Historians figure as many as four hundred thousand cattle were slaughtered by the Gcaleka alone, maybe as many as a million when you add those of the Rarabe and the Thembu groups.

Then the starving and the dying began in an almost unimaginable self-inflicted genocide, the worst to ever beset this country. One does not want to dwell on the details but around seventy thousand people died in the direct aftermath. Those living near enough to the coast resorted to eating shellfish, of which there were plenty but it was taboo food. This practice continues wherever poverty is most keenly felt along the Wild Coast.

The Cape government stepped in assertively, if cynically. Feeding stations would be set up and the Xhosas could get their fill so long as the men signed contracts to indenture them to work on farms, on roads, railways or other arenas of growth in the colony. The old independent Xhosaland, later to be known as the Transkei, was divided into magisterial districts and all power stripped from the chiefs.

Nongqawuse was given up to the colonial authorities and spirited out of the area. She sailed under guard to Cape Town where she was held in custody at a pauper's lodge. She was later released and sent to live on a farm in the Alexandria district, once part of the "disputed territory". She died there some time in the late 1890s or early 1900s.

One policeman who questioned her when she was first detained described her as: "A girl of about sixteen years of age, has a silly look, and appeared to me as if she was not right in her mind. She did not seem to me to take any pains with her appearance."

Her friend Nombanda, when questioned stated: "I frequently accompanied Nongqawuse to a certain bush where she spoke with people – and although she frequently informed me when I was with her at this bush, that she saw people and heard them speak to her – I neither saw them nor did I hear them speak till after I had constantly visited the bush with her."

More than a hundred years later the wheel would turn full circle. Among the first articles of legislation enacted by the ANC government was one that re-instated the power of traditional chiefs, among the ironies of a modern democratic country said to have the most progressive constitution in the world.

I cannot recall when or where I first heard about the Xhosa cattle killing, but it was most likely in high school history lessons. While at Rhodes University I spent most of my holidays exploring the Wild Coast where, on one occasion, local historian Trevor (I forget his surname) took me in his little boat up through "the gates", a dark gorge on the Qolora River. Several hundred metres upstream there was a pool, fed by a waterfall from a higher one. Local lads were jumping the precipice from the one to the other. Trevor told me the pool above was the one where the maiden Nongqawuse had seen her visions more than a century before.

Around that time, 1979, I bought the fabulous book *Myths & Legends of Southern Africa* where it stated that the river in question was the Gxara, and not the Qolora about five kilometres to the north. There was no Google or Google Earth in those days to quickly do a search, but today you can zoom in on the Gxara River on Google Earth and, at a certain resolution, next to Dakeni village you will find a photo image of the pool in question.

If you saunter up the Wild Coast, crossing the Kei River, then the Gxara, the Qolora, Ncizele, Kobonqaba, you will find chiefs sitting in the shade, living on government stipends and ruling over villages that to the eye seem to differ little from the time when Nongqawuse and Nombanda wandered these lovely hills and vales.

The old wounds still run deep there. What can you say other than that, as you sow so shall you reap.

James Stevenson-Hamilton –
Keeper of the Wilderness

The man who really made the Kruger a game reserve

OURS WAS NOT A HOLIDAY-GOING kind of family. The last attempt was a caravanning vacation when I was twelve at a place called Paradise Beach. For us three free-range children it was seaside heaven, but our very urbane parents found it was more like an al fresco Dante's inferno.

The first, a long-weekend visit to the Kruger National Park, went a whole lot better. I think the budget price tag, minimal expectations and the relatively short duration of the trip had something to do with that. Anyways, I was around ten and I fell in love, deeply and irrevocably.

We entered the park at Numbi Gate – every name was like a litany of adventure for me, Numbi, Skukuza, Pretoriuskop, Satara, Letaba – and just inside we saw our first wild animals. Our father stopped the car, turned his head to us three boys sitting excitedly on the back seat of our Hudson Rambler and said in a whisper: "Look closely at those animals boys, it might be the only time you ever see them."

It was a herd of impalas, about as common in the Kruger as feral pigeons in Trafalgar Square. After that it seemed natural that we would see the things we did, like a crowned eagle snatching a vervet monkey from a tree top at Hippo Pools on the Crocodile River while our parents fussed over the picnic table, or the skin of a male lion that a ranger named Harry Wolhuter had killed with his knife.

We stayed in a rondavel in Skukuza rest camp, which to me felt like *Jock of the Bushveld* come to life. I was entranced and bewitched. I was therefore astonished many years later, on reading the autobiography of its first warden James Stevenson-Hamilton, to learn that this wonderland legacy we take so much for granted very nearly did not come into being.

At the end of the Anglo-Boer War in 1902 Major Stevenson-Hamilton was seconded from his regiment, the 6th Inniskilling Dragoons, to attend a new posting as chief ranger of the Sabi Game Reserve. The job description given to him was vague in the extreme: to turn an old hunting ground in the malarial Lowveld into a game sanctuary, but, as this story will elucidate, no one had any idea what that meant.

One of the first characters of the Lowveld with whom Stevenson-Hamilton had to contend was Toothless Jack. He was an ancient African gent who the new warden took on as a member of his unimpressive retinue on the understanding that, having been one of the "hunting boys" of old hunter Henry Glynn Jnr, he would know something of the country into which the newly appointed conservationist and his ragged caravan was headed.

Glynn was one of the legendary hunters who worked the area (in fact what they did was shoot any and every wild animal they could) between the Crocodile and Sabi rivers and deep into Portuguese East Africa. They still mainly used old falling-block rifles with black powder; smokeless powder and magazines only arrived with the Anglo-Boer War.

The warden's party was neither very well provisioned nor manned. They had six emaciated oxen pulling their lone wagon, two unsalted ponies (that is, not immune to horse sickness), a Sotho youth from the Free State who was the driver and horse attendant, a coloured man who was camp attendant, and finally Toothless Jack.

He joined the party in Graskop and at first did not impress, wearing an assemblage of nondescript and "indescribably filthy" garments, but his usefulness soon revealed itself in that he was the only one who could communicate with the local Africans who spoke only Shangaan (otherwise Tonga).

Another notable character was Bill Sanderson, also one of the legendary hunters of the Lowveld. They shot for a living and did not seek out predators since they were interested primarily in meat, skins and ivory. By the time Stevenson-Hamilton arrived to make camp on his farm near White River, the old hunter reckoned elephant, white rhinoceros and eland were locally extinct.

These hunters, Sanderson, Glynn and another, Abel Erasmus, were highly competitive when it came time for telling tales around a fire of their exploits with a gun. Good marksmanship gave one extra boasting rights. The mightily whiskered Sanderson revealed to Stevenson-Hamilton that, as his eyesight began to fade, he employed a particularly sneaky trick whenever he hosted one of his much-coveted hunting parties on his farm.

There were only two rules at these gatherings: you could use only a rifle (no shotguns) and you could shoot at only running antelope. Sanderson had the benefit of a well-trained young gun boy. Whenever Sanderson shot an animal the youth was to steal up to it, then sneak back and tell his employer where the shot had landed. When the group gathered to go and check their quarry, Sanderson would say, for example, "a good shot in the neck" (what he actually said was probably more like "Ay, not a bad yin. I shot yon in the neck").

On reaching his victim the guests would be amazed; how could he tell from two hundred yards where his bullet had hit? To which the wily old Scot would reply that a man ought to hit his target where he had aimed.

On one occasion while visiting Sanderson, founding Kruger Park game ranger Harry Wolhuter decided to sight in a new rifle. He placed an old food tin on a log and took a shot, hitting the can dead centre. Wolhuter suggested that his host also take a shot, an invitation that could not be refused.

When the two men sauntered over to check their handiwork Sanderson commented: "Just as I thought, my shot went clean through the same hole as yours, Harry."

In the first decade after the revival of the Sabi Game Reserve there was precious little game around. The warden and his rangers understood their task was to protect "royal game" – mainly antelope that were the usual targets of sport hunting at the time. Carnivores were to be shot on sight since they preyed on the royal game. Their principle targets were lions, leopards, hyenas and wild dogs. Although all rare at the time, wild dogs, now the most endangered of large carnivores, were then the most plentiful of the carnivorous species.

In the early years Stevenson-Hamilton observed that the wild dogs were highly visible and vocal as well. They would leap above the tall grasses and issue hoarse barks. When they began to be targeted, however, they quickly went to ground.

It was about a decade later that the idea of conserving ecosystems occurred to the warden, and another decade after that, taking Yellowstone Park in the United States as the model, of a park for the people. Conservation for conservation's sake was a concept still far away in the future and there would be many battles ahead before this new-fangled thinking would be accepted.

Stevenson-Hamilton was essentially a soldier, not a hunter, and even less a conservationist, when he took on the task of caretaker of the park. But he understood his role was to protect it from all other interested parties who had their own ideas about what should be done with the place: farmers, miners, hunters, policemen and politicians. In the course of carrying out his self-determined duties he made many enemies. The Scotsman was short in stature but feisty and uncompromising by nature. I would pity anyone who took him on.

No sooner had the country begun to recover from the Anglo-Boer War than hunters, poachers, whatever you care to call them, moved into the area. Stevenson-Hamilton realised what was left of the area's wildlife would not last many more years unless he instituted stringent measures. Also, black people quickly moved in to set up home in the otherwise unoccupied tract where they had once grazed stock seasonally and hunted for the pot.

Among the warden's first tasks was to have them evicted and moved back to their ancestral lands under traditional chiefs. Needless to say, this did not endear him to men like Tshokwane who had designs of establishing himself as a chief in his own right at the picnic spot that bears his name. These evictions, as well as later ones during the tenure of the apartheid government, were the basis of many of the recent land claims in and around the Kruger Park.

This was how his African nickname, Skukuza, came about. It means "he who sweeps clean", referring to Stevenson-Hamilton's unyielding efforts in clearing land invaders and prosecuting poachers.

The warden knew in his heart that he had to – and would have to – protect his chargeling from all comers. Boer hunting parties scoffed at the idea of hunting in the Lowveld. From their point of view the place was already shot out: they were volume consumers and not interested in the elitist notion of hunting for the fun of it, but over the years many individuals and organisations lobbied for the park to be opened for hunting, as well as for the warden to be dismissed.

The magazine *Farmer's Weekly* ran a story 'Scandal of the Sabi Game Reserve' in which it claimed the reserve had become a breeding ground for lions. This had led to a decline in game (that is, "royal game"). The lions should be destroyed and the magazine proposed "sportsmen" be issued with permits to come in and do the dirty work ("someone has to ...").

The idea was roundly supported by the Wild Life Protection Society. One wonders what the current members of the Wildlife and Environment Society of southern Africa would have to say about it. The irony though is that that was precisely what the park rangers had been doing since day one.

Stevenson-Hamilton had to contend with increasing inquiries from government officials to come and see "this game reserve" for themselves. They presumed they would be welcomed and taken on hunting expeditions so were shocked when this was denied them. Whenever the warden received an official order to go out and shoot for the pot for some or other VIP visitors he invariably missed.

Newspaper campaigns were launched to smear Stevenson-Hamilton's name and accuse him of corruption. What else could he and his happy band of rangers be up to in the park into which no one else was allowed! Why, they demanded, had all the lions, wild dogs and crocodiles not been exterminated from the place? Trigger fingers everywhere were getting twitchy.

No one else could fathom his thinking. Once when visiting an old acquaintance, a hotelier in Komatipoort, the man badgered the warden: when was he going to throw open "that reserve of yours" for hunting?

That was the moment, Stevenson-Hamilton recalled in his memoirs, that the conservation penny dropped: "Suddenly I saw myself as the guardian of a trust, and my charge as a little maiden with a possibly important future before her." From thereafter he called the Sabi reserve his Cinderella and, when it morphed into the Kruger National Park, it became his Princess.

However, the journey from serf to royalty would be an even more arduous one than the road taken thus far. More than once Stevenson-Hamilton had to battle for the park's continued future. Time and again, when the feisty park warden stood firm, he found himself losing friends and making enemies in circles low and high. None more so than the time he prosecuted two of the most senior police officers in the Transvaal for poaching and won a conviction against them.

The idea of creating a "game reserve" in the Lowveld had first been mooted in the Transvaal (Zuid-Afrikaansche) Parliament in the 1880s, when Volksraad members from Barberton and Krugersdorp noted the game there, once a stronghold of all Africa's wildest beasts, was disappearing before their eyes.

A proposal came before the Volksraad to close the area between the Crocodile and Sabi rivers as a wild kraal. The area was thick with tsetse flies and malaria and no good for farming anyway, but it took another decade before the idea was adopted, in 1898. War was looming and no gamekeeper was appointed. The following year the Anglo-Boer War broke out.

At the signing of peace in 1902, re-establishing the old Sabi game kraal was a very low priority for the interim Milner government in

Pretoria. However, in their efforts to re-establish the rule of law they sent the mid-level officer (Stevenson-Hamilton) there as a stop-gap measure. How they underestimated their appointee.

Even the veterinarians of the day were strongly opposed to the preservation of wild game areas. Their job was to protect agricultural animals, and wild animals only got in their way. The state vet at the time, a Doctor Viljoen, declared: "All game should be exterminated." They had already all but shot the rhinos from South Africa as well as most of the buffaloes in attempts to eradicate rinderpest, or cattle plague.

Perhaps the time when the park came closest to ceasing to exist was immediately after World War I. The park was opened to stock farmers for grazing. It was extremely hard to keep law and order as the farmers grazed their animals where they pleased, ignored concession boundaries while vying for the best grazing and water, burned the veld and shot game as fast as they could.

Under wartime martial law officials wrote and signed orders for themselves and their friends to shoot in the park. The warden and his rangers, Wolhuter, Fraser, Healey and De la Porte, slept little during that time. They were gloomy days indeed, Stevenson-Hamilton noted, but it was to be the dark before the light of a new era.

Through relentless lobbying he won some powerful friends in the provincial Executive Committee, men like Anglo-Boer War hero Denys Reitz who was minister of lands for the Transvaal and later in the national government. His successor, Piet Grobler, took up the cause of the beleaguered game reserve. They pushed the idea of creating a national park. Staunch conservatives in government pushed back, but the clincher was a masterstroke.

Among the public relations exercises hatched by Stevenson-Hamilton was to bring people into the park by train for them to see the wonders of a healthily preserved and functional savanna ecosystem. They all started out thinking they'd be in for some hunting sports but, by and by, he started winning over – even creating – a league of conservationists. Sir William Hoy, GM of South African Railways, became a powerful voice for the game park cause.

The South African Railways sent an artist to capture the spirit of the place for the rest of the populace to enjoy, and it was he, Stratford Caldecott, who around the camp fire one night suggested that the way to get a national park bill pushed through parliament would be to call it the Kruger National Park. Very few among the previously opposing nationalistic Afrikaner block were going to vote against the greatest hero of Afrikaner cause.

At this point plans were already afoot to host a massive celebration of the centenary of the Great Trek. Minister Piet Grobler, who happened to be a grandnephew of Oom Paul Kruger, lent extra weight to the plight of the game park.

In 1926 the National Parks Act was voted into existence with the Kruger gazetted as the first of its kind in Africa. Actually, the first national park in Africa was the Parc National des Virungas, established in the Belgian Congo (now the DRC) in 1925 to protect mountain gorillas. However, the high-altitude montane forest ecosystem is not a game reserve in the traditional sense.

In truth Paul Kruger, president of the Transvaal Republic, was no lion hugger. He never personally supported the idea of a Lowveld "wild kraal" and three times he and his old hunting comrades in arms voted down the proposal. Still, more than a century later, the name survives as the brand of the world's most famous and most visited game reserve in South Africa, probably all of Africa, possibly the whole world.

That, however, was not the end of the learning curve for the park, for along with national park status came a mandate to open it to the public. For the first few years no facilities whatsoever were provided. Visitors had to camp, stretching tarpaulins between cars, and they had to carry firearms for protection. Entry cost £1 a car. Only three cars entered in 1927.

Swapping parcels of land, mainly with mining houses, the park was greatly expanded northwards, first to the Shingwedzi and thereafter to the Pafari-Levuvhu River (the expansion to the Limpopo came only in the early 1970s). This was done, however, at the expense of relinquishing some more fertile lands to the west. Higher ground towards the escarpment would have provided vital seasonal variation of habitats and rainfall for the game, but you win some you lose some. It might yet come to pass.

Pretoriuskop was the first rest camp to open, with just several rondavels offering … not very much at all. Stevenson-Hamilton and his rangers had roughed it out there for nearly three decades. They did not want visitors lounging around in comfortable rest camps so facilities were kept Spartan in the extreme, encouraging guests to head out at first light into the park. It worked.

By 1930 five more rest camps had been established, Skukuza, Satara, Letaba, Olifants and Shingwedzi. The rest is history: there are now around 24 public rest camps and about as many private game lodges. During World War II the park was closed to visitors and most of the rangers enlisted for active service. On their return in 1946 Stevenson-Hamilton decided it was time to move on and out.

"I had at least brought up Cinderella and launched her on her career. I loved her best when she was a pathetic and dust-covered little wench, derided and abused. Now she has become a Great Lady it was fitting she be provided with custodians perhaps better suited to provide her new requirements."

Stevenson-Hamilton descended from a long and distinguished line of high-ranking army officers, but this Scottish soldier was also a talented artist who looked very closely at the world around him. From the age of twelve he kept a personal illustrated diary. From his first to his last day in the park he made daily entries about the animals, weather conditions, human interactions and political intrigues. He was an astute observer of nature and he ran the park along rigorous scientific principles that have been maintained to this day.

However, should the uncompromising old warden return today he might be aghast at the unlimited luxury offered at some of the modern private safari lodges in the park, but things change and clearly they better suit the new requirements of twenty-first-century tourism.

The next time you visit the Kruger National Park take some time to climb Shirimantanga Koppie, the highest and most prominent point in the southern section of the park. It was where the prince of South African conservation loved to gaze upon his realm and contemplate things as they were and as they might have been. It is where his ashes were scattered.

The epitaph "if you seek his monument look around you" was first assigned to Sir Christopher Wren, the architect tasked with rebuilding London after the "great fire" of 1666. It is an equally fitting one for James Stevenson-Hamilton. We, and all the creatures great and small that live in or visit the Kruger Park, owe him much.

The Gang That Lost its Shoes

Botswana's wildlife warriors take no prisoners

AT ITS MOST BASIC, THIS IS A STORY about crime and punishment, with an epilogue that might suggest divine intervention. In any fight not everyone always agrees who are the bad guys and who are the good, what is right and what is wrong. In a conflict where land rights, rural subsistence, environmental sustainability and general enrichment are set against one another the battle lines tend to be blurred.

As long as *Homo sapiens* ruled the savanna we have hunted and gathered. For centuries, millennia, the balance held, where indigenous communities and wildlife skirted one another with wary respect. For just as long the elements were held in balance in a magnificent and indifferent diorama, but some time around mid-last century, scenes of this Pleistocene Eden started fading like the final credits in a movie entitled *This Was the Africa We Knew*.

In truth the stone that caused the very first ripples of paradigm change here in southern Africa was the fall of Constantinople to the Ottoman horde in 1453. After a thousand years of dominance, Europe's financial link to the East, the Silk Road, was constricted.

The kingdoms and principalities that depended on that trade needed to find an alternative route or face economic strangulation. Sailing ships departed from Lisbon and Palos, Marseilles and Hamburg, Amsterdam and London began to disgorge the hungry vanguards of religion, commerce and conquest on the beaches of Africa.

With a steady march beachheads became settlements and settlements became colonies. With the planting of flags and loading of cannons the old authority of chiefs was usurped by pale-skinned, pith-helmeted bureaucrats. With a mere stroke of a pen, game-rich areas became designated game reserves, hunting became poaching and hunter became hounded.

Hunting for survival was outlawed in order to facilitate hunting for sport. Little wonder that those who stole out in the darkness to bring back meat for the table were admired and protected – African Robin Hoods – then as much as now. Where you stood in this brave new world depended on which side of the socio-economic current your hut was located.

Most poaching has always been simply for food, but there was always better bread at the luxury goods end of the supply chain – elephant foot ashtray stands, rhino horn trinkets, ivory piano keys, love potions. The animals were plentiful and dangerous. People were few and rusty weapons were as dangerous to the hunter as the hunted. The next paradigm shift was in weaponary, from front loading to breech loading rifles at the end of the nineteenth century; the one after that the rise of Asian economies in the second half of the twentieth century.

Wherever there is a buck to be made you will find prospectors, extractors, financiers, dealers and wheelers. It is no mystery that wherever you find Chinese road builders, dam makers and traders there you will also find elephants, rhinos, pangolins, gorillas – everything and anything saleable or edible – appear on the market. For the past few decades China has been buying up Africa lock, stock and two smoking barrels. In this time the number of African elephants has been chopped down from more than a million to fewer than four hundred and fifty thousand, a loss of around sixty-five per cent.

In the case of black rhinos the statistics are changing daily but their numbers plummeted from around seventy thousand to fewer than two thousand five hundred – three per cent – in just the past few decades. Southern white rhino populations were historically much smaller and the southern race was very nearly made extinct by the end of the nineteenth century. There are now thought to be around twenty thousand (most of them in South Africa) but the northern race is now believed to be extinct.

Of course you knew all this, more or less, but along with rising stakes there has developed an arms race between poachers and conservationists. The days of poachers wielding bows and spears are long over, along with flushing out poachers with small rewards.

Modern-day poaching gangs are armed and paid by middlemen who represent criminal syndicates, mainly in East Asia, with enormously deep pockets. The money is good enough to kill for or to die for. They will shoot before they surrender. It's a war and, as in all wars, the worst hit are those caught in the middle, in this case the animals.

In 1990 the last black rhino living wild in Botswana was killed in the Saile Forest Reserve. Shot by poachers in the Kwando-Linyanti wetlands, the point of wilderness where the Caprivi Strip sticks its Namibian thumb down into Botswana. It's just a hop across the river for Namibian poaches, and a skip and a hop for any from markets in Angola, Zimbabwe and Zambia.

This incident galvanised the country into serious action. General (later President) Ian Khama, head of the army back then and eldest son of the country's first president Sir Seretse Khama, called in the big guns. He put together a small anti-poaching unit within the country's defence force that could be choppered in whenever a serious poaching incident had been reported. They began to have some successes, mainly by removing snares and generally being a well-armed and trained presence.

As the scale of poaching there became evident, the small anti-poaching unit grew into a nine-hundred-strong special forces corps, but still the mostly town-born soldiers, with little or no real experience with wild game, were no match for the bush-wise poachers. This was a new kind of war for the Botswana Defence Force (BDF). Armies are good at defending towns and trenches, but how do you defend the wilderness?

They were trained to get along with elephants that wanted their share of the water in the army camps, familiarised their patrol horses with lions and were trained to handle deadly snakes – no dog walk for people with a traditional terror of snakes. You would find it hilarious watching the soldiers as a large spitting cobra slithered over polished boots and crawled around pressed trouser legs, standing dead still with death-mask grimaces.

By and by the entire BDF morphed from a conventional army into Africa's most efficient band of wildlife warriors.

Living and working in the bush, this new generation of gun-toting, camo-fatigued nature champions began to turn the tide on poaching, but still the elephants and other game in the Saile Forest area were being relentlessly targeted. Once the rhino horn was exhausted, elephant ivory became the target, along with hippo ivory and meat destined for food markets to the north. Shooting hippos in their pools was like shooting cows in a field. Even elephants stood no chance against the new heavy firepower of commercial poachers.

Loopholes in Botswana's laws were tightened. Lion hunting was banned and then restrictions were placed on sport hunting for elephants. Citizen hunting, an easy out for any poacher, was discontinued. The soldiers were instructed to shoot to kill whenever necessary: the first time such a command had ever been issued from the top. No prisoners, no excuses, no regrets: this was a matter of protecting the country's vital resources.

Every time an elephant carcass was found the trackers would be called in. Combined with mounted patrols the soldiers could cover large areas, but time and again the trail of the poachers vanished into dust and across the water into the lawless Caprivi Strip.

The poaching arms race was notched up with helicopters and horse patrols joined by foot patrols and motorboat sorties, and one by one the poaching gangs in northern Botswana were stymied, apprehended, arrested, shot – except for the poachers of the Saile Forest, phantom figures seemingly beyond physical restraint.

For the rangers it became increasingly harrowing to find that they were always just too late and then powerless: elephant carcasses were riddled with fire from automatic weapons, the tusks savagely chopped off, an animal bled out, one foot sliced off by a wire snare, another elephant trying to revive its dead comrade, the anxiety palpable as it tried to raise the dead animal with its tusks. The soldiers felt impotent against a ghostly foe that left no detectable trail.

One day a foot patrol walked into a poachers' camp, the entire area hanging heavy with drying meat but no one home. A night ambush was set using night-vision scopes. The gang returned under cover of darkness on a moonless night, flush from a big delivery. In the ensuing gunfight some of the poachers were killed, the rest apprehended.

When the camp was searched by daylight it was found that the gang had left their working shoes behind in camp. Riempie straps attached the dinner plate-sized soles of dried out elephant feet. The secret of the disappearing poachers of Saile was finally revealed: all the time the soldiers had been following phantom pachyderms.

This story of poaching and anti-poaching is covered in the movie *Wildlife Warriors* by Dereck and Beverly Joubert. I visited them at their simple tent camp in the wild Linyanti region of northern Botswana during my years working at *Getaway* magazine. We spoke of this and many other of their amazing adventures while compiling their numerous award-winning films. It amused me that Dereck would go jogging in the middle of the day ("best time, predators are mostly sleeping") carrying just a stick.

Walking (or jogging) around the bush on one's own became second nature. This was where, some three decades later, they were walking to dinner in their camp, and an old buffalo charged at close quarters out of the darkness. These old bulls that have been pushed out of their herd and left to the mercy of predators are called "dhaga boys" because they spend most of their time mud bathing and are usually covered in clay, or dhaga. They are the most feared of all the so-called "big five".

It hit Dereck first, smashing into his ribs and breaking his pelvis. Then it swung its enormous boss at Beverly, gouging her under the armpit, impaling her and swinging her into the air like a limp doll. One horn went through her entire body, up through her throat and out her cheek.

In an interview Dereck later recalled: "The buffalo had a wound, ironically almost a mirror image of Beverly's, from another buffalo, into its lung. When I was knocked down, I got up and ran after the buffalo (with Beverly impaled) and landed one kick in its side. By chance I kicked near enough to its wound that it burst open and it was possibly that action that turned the buffalo, made him flick Beverly off and release her, and ultimately saved her."

Although Beverly sustained a collapsed lung and suffered through many hours of surgery to reconstruct bone damage, muscles and nerves, the horn missed her spine, her heart, oesophagus, arteries, optic nerve and her eye – all by millimetres.

And so to add to their many awards and "war medals" that have included several bouts of malaria, three plane crashes, three deadly snake bites, four serious elephant attacks and umpteen scorpion stings (they will if you walk around the bush in sandals), they now have what was described on their Facebook page as a "buffalo smack down". *Poachers beware; these conservationists won't be easily stopped.*

The Zeederberg Express
– Southern Africa's Most
Illustrious Mail Service

Divas, desperadoes and dignitaries

MY FRIEND DONALD inducted me into the Dangerous Sports Club when I was ten or so. Go-carts were overridden by motorbikes, snorkeling superseded by spearfishing, rock climbing voided by paragliding and that in turn dismounted by mountain biking (with a few other dips into danger along the way). The search for increasingly dangerous places to ride our bicycles led us to Mashatu Private Game Reserve in Botswana's savage Tuli Block.

Some of the paths we rode, we discovered, had first been gouged into the veld by the wheels of the coaches of the Zeederberg Express, which ferried all manner of people as well as bullion between the gold fields of Matabeleland and The Reef. Pont Drift, Bryce's Store and Fort Jameson were waypoints on the coach route within the Tuli area. At some point it occurred to me that, among the rows of dusty second-hand books I'd collected over the years, many of them still unread, was one by Harry, a member of the famous Zeederberg family, who had penned the story of their illustrious transport business.

We have returned to Mashatu many times to ride those trails and it never ceases to thrill me to know we are riding down tracks of history. I've seen old cartridges and flattened bully beef cans among the bits of yesterday scattered around where Bryce's Store – one of the staging posts for the mail service – used to stand. It was flattened by a well-placed Boer artillery shell during the South African War of 1899–1902; turns out Mr Bryce was smuggling arms to the British forces holed up inside Fort Tuli in what is now Zimbabwe.

When I did finally get round to reading the book in question, I found it to be as rollicking an adventure as was ever written about this part of the world in days long gone. If you were born between the mid-1950s and 1960s (as was I) your grandparents probably saw the biggest technological changes of any generation in the whole history of humankind, fire and wheels notwithstanding.

Most likely they went to school by ox-wagon or horse cart, courted in a Model-T Ford, went on family holidays by steam train and listened to the radio when Neil Armstrong stepped onto the moon (no TV in South Africa in those days, it was deemed too revolutionary by the jowl-faced keepers of the apartheid fortress).

They – your grandparents that is – would have been familiar with coach services like the Zeederberg Express, not the only ones active across the wide, wild southern African veld in those days but definitely the most enduring and successful of them all. There were, in all, twenty-nine coaching companies operating at one time or another.

The Zeederberg service was started by brothers Louw and Pieter to carry supplies by ox-wagon during the Anglo-Zulu War, later between the burgeoning centres of southern Africa. At that time Geo. Heys & Co. dominated coach travel, the main line being that between the diamond fields at Kimberley and Pretoria, while the Red Star Line operated from the Boer capital to the gold rush towns of Pilgrim's Rest, Barberton and Kaapsche Hoop.

With the gold business seeming to be a sure-bet bull market, the Zeederbergs decided to expand. Their big break came in securing a monopoly from Cecil John Rhodes to run the "hunter's road" from

Pretoria, across the great grey-green, greasy Limpopo River into Bechuanaland, shortly thereafter across the wide Shashe to the new gold fields in what was then called Zambesia but soon was to be renamed Rhodesia. The local Africans called the route pandamatenga, pick up and carry, because inevitably it was they who ended up doing all the lifting and carrying.

There was the self-styled and probably dyslexic highwayman Dick Terpend who enjoyed several bountiful years on the road here in the 1880s to contend with, as well as the usual lion attacks, elephants destroying camps and overturning wagons, crocodiles in the Limpopo River taking mules and the usual rainstorms, river floods and stuck-in-the-mud stoppages.

Many drivers considered a trip to be little more than a fully paid hunting expedition, but it was not all fun, camp fires and big game. Coaches were washed away in floods, passengers had to ride mules out of swamps, gold bars "fell" out of coaches and at times the drivers and passengers together had to fight off hordes of spear-wielding attackers.

Many wheels were broken when a driver failed to notice a donga, the knee-deep water gullies that run downhill across paths and roads just about everywhere across the veld. Just a momentary lapse by the driver and a wagon wheel would be eaten up by the gaping yaw of a donga. It was all in a day's work on the Zeederberg Coach Line.

At one time a visiting cricket team from England had to be transported to Bulawayo and back to Park Station in Johannesburg. Opera and theatre companies would tour from the Cape to Mashonaland, riding on top of boxes filled with bullion on heavily overloaded wagons and coaches.

In 1899, after a period of thrust and parry (thrusting at diamonds, parrying for gold), war broke out between Boer and Brit all around South Africa and the adjoining parcels of land, including the Tuli Block in what are today southeastern Botswana and southwestern Zimbabwe. Just about everyone got entangled in the fray.

Cecil John Rhodes commissioned the Zeederberg coaches to carry troops and arms down from Bulawayo to reinforce the British garrison at Fort Tuli on the Shashe River, close to the current Botswana-Zimbabwe-South African convergence. Meanwhile the Boers had taken up position on a low dolerite ridge on the northern side of Nel's Vlei (in Botswana) just within sight of the fort (inside Zimbabwe).

The two sides got locked in a stand-off of artillery bombardments and sniper fire, much to the astonishment of the wild animals, you can bet. Spent shell and rifle cartridge cases can still be found around the vlei, as well as bits and pieces around Bryce's Store.

The stagecoach business relied on horses and mules but the attrition rate was so high, with African horse sickness a plague on the land. At one time the Zeederberg company experimented with using zebras to pull the coaches. Zebras seemed to be immune to horse sickness but there were a few other problems. Unlike horses and mules, zebras are wild and never easily tamed. It is true that by and by they were tamed well enough for circus acts or to pull wagons, but not for very long.

First thing, though, is that you had to start by catching some wild zebras. Following a long period of breaking in and training young zebras that had been born in captivity from captured animals, the company tried them on a few short trips. It seemed to work so well that they ventured to test a zebra span on the long haul all the way from Pretoria to Bulawayo. The thing was, so they learned, that while zebras could run nearly as fast as a horse, they could not run nearly as far. It was a disaster.

In February of 1893 a large crowd gathered in Pretoria to give a rousing cheer to the first coach carrying ten passengers pulled by a team of nine zebras and one mule as the lead animal, with chief driver Jock Bannatyne at the reins. The coach proceeded down Potgieter Street and past Church Square and even the president of the Transvaal Republic came out onto his stoep to witness the commotion.

"It is an evil day when wild animals are made to do the work which the Almighty has ordained should be done by domestic animals", the heavily lidded and even more heavily bearded old Bible thumper is recorded to have said.

Maybe the Almighty himself was observing all the palaver from his omniscient cloud because just about everything that could go wrong did. An axle broke when a wheel hit a pothole while Bannatyne was dozing besides his co-driver Daniel Letsoala (in coaching parlance the runciman, the one who holds the horses and then makes a running leap aboard as the coach takes off), a promising young Sotho lad doing his apprenticeship under the dour Scotsman.

With the younger man nursing a size twelve boot impression on his backside, the older man rode the mule back to Pretoria to fetch a new axle. It took some hours before the new part was in place, by which time it was dark and drivers and passengers had to spend the night in the coach (something not unheard of during those times).

From Pretoria the wagon road passed through Warmbad where the passengers enjoyed a bathe in the hot mineral spring (the local Africans called it Bela-Bela, implying a pot that boils). Thus refreshed they continued on to Nylstroom which had been named by the Voortrekkers when, seeking a new Canaan (the land of milk and honey) and encountering the first river flowing northwards, they assumed they had reached the fabled Nile. A rounded hill they took to be a ruined Pyramid. The local Africans called it Modimolle ("the spirits of the ancestors have eaten").

Next came Naboomspruit, named after the grotesque succulent euphorbia trees of the region. The African name from them is mokgopa. From the place of giant succulent trees they passed Potgietersrus where any Afrikaans speakers among the passengers would doff their hats to the Boer women and children whose heads had been bashed against the trunks of large camelthorn trees that lined the track. The women and children had been left behind in a fortified wagon laager while the men went off on horseback in pursuit of Mzilikazi's impi that was marauding through the area. The Ndebele leader's men found them hiding in the grove of acacia trees where the main road north later ran.

The local Africans called the place Mokopane, after the chief who sought shelter in the extensive cave system nearby while evading first Mzilikazi's hordes and later a Boer commando. The Boers had cannons into which they loaded pepper-filled shells and bombarded the caves. When the occupants emerged, spewing red pepper from their lungs, they were picked off by Boer marksmen.

The next day the coach passed through Pietersburg, which the local Africans knew as Polokwane ("place of safety" as it was renamed in due course), with much the same fanfare as had seen them off in Pretoria. From there the wagon road veered to the northwest, passing between the Waterberg and Soutpansberg ranges on its way to Rhodes Drift (now called Pont Drift) on the Limpopo River.

Approaching the big river the road proved to be treacherous as there had been heavy rains the previous week. They had just crossed the drift where large pools of water still lay in the river bed and the going underfoot was exceedingly squelchy. Bannatyne was driving when the coach slid off the road.

Going up the incline of the far side the draught animals could not get good purchase on the slippery mud. The driver made the foolish mistake of trying to whip the span into shape, which had the opposite effect and zebras, mule, coach, occupants and drivers slid slowly off the road and found themselves sitting axle deep in an oozing swamp. This time young Daniel was sent off to Bryce's Store for help, where there would be a new draught team waiting for them. He returned some hours later with fresh animals to pull them out.

Another night was spent sleeping on the road rather than the warm comfort of the basic but still warm lodgings at the store, and that was when the lions attacked. Bannatyne and Letsoala managed to let off a few rounds each from their Martini-Henry rifles and drive off the fearsome beasts, but not before one zebra had been killed and two others mauled so badly they had to be dispatched on the spot.

The nervous passengers helped collect wood to make a fire and then took turns keeping watch through the rest of the night. When another wagon, drawn by mules, with only three passengers on board, stopped to view the wreckage the next morning, bidding was furious for the seven vacant seats to Bryce's Store, Fort Tuli and thence on to Bulawayo. And that was pretty much the end of Operation Zebra.

In order to implement Rhodes's dream of, if not a road all the way from the Cape to Cairo, then at least a coach route to Victoria Falls, labour gangs were recruited to make a passable road. While pushing the route onwards from the Limpopo, across the Pitsani (which had to be crossed several times) and the Shashe, elephants and lions were constant threats.

On one occasion in 1890 when a group of elephants approached from out the riverine thicket, the workers began throwing stones at them. This was unusual behaviour because normally the people would continue working and the elephants move away. They noted a white hunter in camp and spied a chance to get fresh meat. The elephants trumpeted and charged and the workers threw down their picks and shovels and ran to the safety of the armed supervisor. In fact, the workers had decided they fancied some elephant meat and so provoked the charge. What they didn't know was that their white "hunter" had never before shot game. He tried to divert the pachyderms by rushing towards them on his horse then veering away.

It worked for three of them but a fourth elephant set upon trashing the supply wagons. The wagon driver, Louw Zeederberg, had also never shot big game but was determined to save his train and so fired at the elephant. The animal turned and trumpeted off into the bush, apparently wounded. That evening two renowned elephant hunters Josias Grobler and Hans Duvenhage, rode into camp.

In the morning the labourers refused to take up their tools so the two ivory hunters were persuaded to track down and finish off the wounded animal. Some days later the hunters returned to the work camp carrying two large tusks. The meat was greatly enjoyed by villagers in the area but nothing was forthcoming for the workers who had set the plan into action.

Next into camp, riding just ahead of approaching summer rains, was another hunter, Randolph Teale, who agreed to halt his journey in order to shoot game to feed the work force. One afternoon while out hunting, Theale came across a pride of lions and fired, wounding one of them. He followed the blood trail into the thicket and before he could lift his rifle the lion attacked. When his gun bearer followed up they found the lion feasting on the hunter.

Roads were at best rocky, rugged or muddy. The year 1887 was a particularly wet one. A coach from Durban got bogged down in thick clay mud in Booysens, then a mining camp just south of Ferreirastown, later Johannesburg. In pouring rain the driver, his assistant and the passengers, nine men and three women, could not move the mired coach. The team was outspanned, each horse or mule was saddled with just a wet blanket and so the passengers rode into town.

Among them was Alma Obrey, a famous vaudeville actress who was due on the stage at the Empire Theatre that night. She rode up to the Grand National Hotel where she was billeted, dismounted and trailed a watery path to the reception desk where she stated simply – with a crowd now gathered – "my name is Miss Obrey, my key please." The hotelier Oscar Schmidt, specifically there to meet and greet her, handed her the key without saying a word.

Half an hour later she tread a royal path through the gathered crowd to take the waiting cab to the theatre. Obrey was for a time one of the highest paid actresses in the world, what with all that gold washing around the "ridge of white waters". By and by she settled down in Johannesburg and married one of the fabulously wealthy Rand Lords.

In June 1891 the coach company received a telegram from Cecil John Rhodes, to convey Sir Randolph Churchill, father of Winston, from the Witwatersrand gold fields to Zambesia. By accounts, Sir Randolph was not impressed by the small towns he passed through. In Vryburg, while he was ensconced at Pullen's Hotel (it was reputedly one of the finest hostelries in the coach route) smoking an imported cigar on the verandah he was overheard to exclaim "what a d... country!" Dashed, damnable, dastardly, one wonders?

Later he found the board to be even more dismal or dastardly than the lodgings. "It's disgraceful, even for a semi-civilised country", he told his table companions on reading the menu. This is what he would have read:

Soup (oyster or egg)
Chicken pie
Jaleme (curry and rice)
Roast leg of mutton
Saleme (duck with mint sauce)
Lamb (with mint sauce)
Corned mutton
Saddle of mutton
Boiled mutton
Stuffed roast turkey
Stuffed roast duck (with mushrooms)

Roast fowl
Boiled fowl (with caper sauce)
Boiled corned beef
Boiled ham
Roast and boiled potatoes and beans

For dessert:
Boiled currant pudding (with wine sauce)
Fruit pie
Red currant pie (with custard)
Tipsy cake
Cake a'merengue
Custard tart
Plain tart
Queen's tart
Fruit a la merengue
Blanc mange
Jams, raisins and almonds

Cheeses, expensive wines and cigars were laid on courtesy of the proprietor, George Pullen. It certainly sounds good enough for royalty visiting a semi-civilised country, but apparently not so for Randy. Writing to a friend back in England he noted: "Having had to partake of these dishes, I can truthfully say that I would have given a gold mine in Mashonaland for a quarter of an hour at the Atheneum."

Flat meat and two veg for you then, your lordship!

I bought my secondhand copy of Harry Zeederberg's book for R250 from Rattlesnake Books in Muizenberg (named after HMS *Rattlesnake*, one of the big guns when the British invaded the Cape in 1795). On opening it I found a telegram tucked into the front dustjacket. It was dated 6 October 1972 and read: "Mr Wingate-Pearse 145 High Level Road = Congratulations on your centenary God bless fond memories = Tilly Ackhurst +".

Mr Wingate-Pearse would have been born in 1872. I'll bet he saw some remarkable changes in his lifetime.

Companion Reading List

Harry Wolhuter

Memoirs of a Game Ranger by Harry Wolhuter (Wildlife and Protection Society of South Africa, 1948; Collins/Fontana Books, London, 1971)

Anthony Hall-Martin

Elephants of Africa by Anthony Hall Martin and Paul Bosman (C Struik, Cape Town, 1986)

Krotoa

Time Longer Than Rope by Eddie Roux (The University of Wisconsin Press, London, 1948, 1964)

Claude Finch-Davies

Claude Gibney Finch-Davies by Alan Kemp (Transvaal Museum, Pretoria, 1976)

The Birds of Southern Africa by Claude Gibney Finch-Davies (illustrations) and Dr Alan Kemp (text) (Winchester Press, Johannesburg, 1982)

Maria Mouton

First Fifty Years by Mansell Upham (Facebook page)

In the Heart of the Country, by JM Coetzee (Martin Secker & Warburg, London, 1977)

Rogues, Rebels and Runaways by Nigel Penn (David Philip, Cape Town, 1999)

Coenraad De Buys

Coenrad de Buys: The First Transvaler by Agatha Elizabeth Schoeman (University of Pretoria/JH de Bussy, Pretoria, 1938)

Frontiers by Noël Mostert (Jonathan Cape, 1992)

King of the Bastards by Sarah Gertrude Millin (Heinemann, 1950)

Dart & Boshier

The Lightning Bird by Lyall Watson (EP Dutton, New York, 1982)

David Livingstone

David Livingstone: The Truth Behind the Legend by Rob Mackenzie (Figtree, Chinhoyi, 1993)

Dr James Barry

Dr James Barry: A Woman Ahead of Her Time by Michael du Preez and Jeremy Dronfield (Oneworld, London, 2016)

Grow Lovely, Growing Old: The Story of Cape Town's Three Centuries by Lawrence G Green (Howard Timmins, Cape Town, undated, reprinted 1975)

Eugéne Marais

Soul of the White Ant by Eugéne N Marais (Methuen & Co, London, 1937)

The Dark Stream/Die Groot Verlange by Leon Rousseau (Jonathan Ball, 1999)

George Mossop

Running the Gauntlet by George Mossop (Thomas Nelson and Sons, London, undated; GC Button, Pietermaritzburg, 1990)

James Kitching

Life Etched in Stone: Fossils of South Africa by Colin MacRae (The Geological Society of South Africa, Johannesburg, 1999)

The True Story of Earth & Life by Bruce Rubidge and Terence McCarthy (Struik/New Holland, Cape Town, 2005)

Nongqawuse

Myths & Legends of Southern Africa by Penny Miller (TV Bulpin, 1979)

James Stevenson-Hamilton

Jock of the Bushveld by Sir Percy Fitzpatrick (Longmans, Green & Co, London, 1907; Puffin/Penguin Books, Johannesburg, 1976)

South African Eden: The Kruger National Park by James Stevenson-Hamilton (Casssel & Co, 1937; Struik, 1993)

Zeederberg

Veld Express by H Zeederberg (Howard Timmins, Cape Town, 1971)